Hildegard Kühne

Analysis and recognition of human actions with flow features and temporal models

Analysis and recognition of human actions with flow features and temporal models

by
Hildegard Kühne

Scientific Publishing

Dissertation, Karlsruher Institut für Technologie (KIT)
Fakultät für Informatik, 2014
Tag der mündlichen Prüfung: 4. Juli 2014
Referenten: Prof. Dr. Rainer Stiefelhagen, Prof. Dr. Rüdiger Dillmann

Impressum

KIT Scientific Publishing

Karlsruher Institut für Technologie (KIT)
KIT Scientific Publishing
Straße am Forum 2
D-76131 Karlsruhe

KIT Scientific Publishing is a registered trademark of Karlsruhe Institute of Technology. Reprint using the book cover is not allowed.

www.ksp.kit.edu

Print on Demand 2015

ISBN 978-3-7315-0282-1
DOI 10.5445/KSP/1000043583

Abstract

Parallel to the growing amount of video data recorded and distributed by smart phones, media companies and surveillance cameras, the automatic classification of short human actions as well as the parsing of complex activities in videos has become a popular research subject in the field of computer vision. But as techniques for the classification of actions in predefined video clips become more and more sophisticated, the parsing and analysis of longer activities that are made up of different smaller motion entities is still in the beginning.

This work focuses on the last point, the analysis and recognition of complex human activities in video data. A combination of new features as well as the application of techniques from speech recognition is proposed to realize a recognition of action units and their combinations in video sequences. The here presented flow features are based on sleek, but powerful video based motion representations. To build flow features, optical flow information is interpolated and concatenated over time corresponding to a representation of the ongoing motion. In the presented system the features are used for a frame wise encoding of the overall video.

Further, to address the problem of analyzing and segmenting complex activity sequences techniques from the domain of speech recognition are made available for the case of video analysis. It is assumed that activities are made up of small undividable low level entities, so called action units that can be concatenated to longer sequences of activities. To model action recognition as a structured temporal process, an open source automated speech recognition engine, the Hidden Markov Model Tool Kit (HTK) is used. Concepts from speech recognition can be naturally transferred to activity recognition: Coarsely labeled action units, modeled by Hidden Markov Models (HMMs) and much like words in speech, form the building blocks for longer activity sequences. Units are combined into sequences using an action grammar. Beside action recognition, this approach enables the semantic parsing as well as the segmentation of videos at the level of single frames.

Further, there is also a need for suitable training and evaluation data. One limitation associated with the use of HMMs for action recognition is that they require large amounts of training data. Additionally, most action recognition datasets lack annotations for basic atomic entities within individual sequences, which are needed to train temporal models like HMMs. To address this point three different datasets have been build and/or annotated, among them one of the largest datasets for human activity parsing and segmentation, the Breakfast dataset comprising 10 distinct cooking activities, each conducted by 52 unique participants in 18 different kitchens. Within all datasets action units like "pour milk" or "take plate" have been manually annotated. This broad annotation on unit level allows for the first time to evaluate action recognition algorithms regarding those intensely discussed problems.

Finally, this work evaluates the proposed feature type and recognition technique, as well as their corresponding state-of-the-art reference methods on all three datasets. Therefore, different accuracy measurements have to be taken into account: the sequence accuracy, that evaluates the recognition of the overall video clip and that is comparable to reported benchmark results, the unit accuracy, that measures how many units were recognized correctly and is an indication for the parsing quality, and the frame accuracy, that measures how many frames were associated with the correct action unit and is thus, a measurement for the correctness of the segmentation. Evaluation shows that the system allows analyzing video content over time on a level of detail which cannot be provided by other systems so far. Additionally, it is superior to global action recognition the longer and more complex the sequences become.

The following work shows how motion information gained from video data can be used to understand and interpret the underlying structural information of actions. It is hoped that the presented approach provides a first step towards higher level models that allow an abstraction of different motion categories beyond simple classification.

Zusammenfassung

Die Wahrnehmung und Interpretation menschlicher Bewegungen ist eine zentrale Fähigkeit des Menschen. Sie ist grundlegender Bestandteil menschlicher Kommunikation und erlaubt es Handlungen und Absichten des Gegenübers zu erkennen, neue Bewegungen zu erlernen und komplexe Situation wie z.B. den Straßenverkehr oder auch die Handlung eines Theaterstücks zu erfassen. Mit der zunehmenden Menge digitaler Videoinformation, die zum großen Teil auch Menschen in den verschiedensten Situationen erfasst, steigt auch das Interesse, diese bisher nur indirekt in Form von Pixeln vorliegende Information automatisch auszuwerten. Nicht zuletzt aus dieser Motivation heraus hat sich die automatische Erkennung und Klassifikation menschlicher Bewegungen zu einem der populären Forschungsthemen der letzten Jahre entwickelt. Hierbei haben sich vor allem Techniken für die Klassifikation einzelner Bewegungen in kurzen Videoclips herausgebildet. Die zeitliche, semantische und syntaktische Analyse längerer Aktivitäten kann dem entgegen als ein eher neues Feld im Bereich der videobasierten Bewegungserkennung angesehen werden. Die folgende Arbeit beschäftigt sich mit letzterer Fragestellung, der Analyse und Erkennung komplexer, zielgerichteter Aktivitäten in Videos.

Dazu werden neue, videobasierte Merkmale in Kombination mit bereits bewährten Techniken aus dem Bereich der automatische Spracherkennung vorgestellt, die es ermöglichen kleine Bewegungseinheiten sowie deren zeitliche Verkettung zu erkennen und zu analysieren. Diese sogenannten Flussmerkmale stellen einfache, aber entscheidende Bewegungsinformationen innerhalb des Videoclips dar. Sie basieren auf dem optischen Fluss einen Videos, der über mehrere Frames zusammengesetzt und interpoliert wird.

Die zusammengesetzten Bewegungsvektoren bilden ein Flussmerkmal, welches die aktuelle Bewegung an dieser Stelle des Videos wiedergibt. Die Flussmerkmale werden im Folgenden genutzt, um die Bewegungsinformation innerhalb des Videos auf Frameebene zu quantifizieren. Dazu wurden verschiedenen Techniken evaluiert, wobei die sogenannte Bag-of-words Methode die besten Erkennungsergebnisse erzielt.

Um darüber hinaus komplexe Aktivitäten in Videos analysieren und erkennen zu können, wurden Elemente aus dem Bereich der automatischen Spracherkennung auf den Bereich der videobasierten Bewegungserkennung übertragen. Dazu wird zunächst angenommen, dass komplexere Tätigkeiten aus kleinen, unteilbaren Einheiten bestehen, die sich zu längeren Sequenzen zusammensetzen lassen. Um eine Erkennung auf Basis eines strukturierten Prozesses über die Zeit zu ermöglichen, wurde das Open source System HTK (Hidden Markov Model Tool Kit) an die Bedürfnisse der videobasierten Bewegungserkennung angepasst. Dabei können die Konzepte der Sprachverarbeitung direkt auf die Probleme der videobasierten Bewegungserkennung übertragen werden: Kleinere Bewegungseinheiten, die im Prinzip den Wörtern einer Sprache entsprechen werden mit Hidden Markov Modellen (HMMs) abgebildet. Sie sind die grundlegenden Bausteine für komplexere Aktivitäten und können mit Hilfe von Bewegungsgrammatiken zu längeren Sequenzen zusammengesetzt werden um längere Tätigkeiten zu erkennen und die Analyse komplexer Aktivitäten zu ermöglichen.

Darüber hinaus beschäftigt sich diese Arbeit auch mit der Frage, welche Daten für das Training und die Evaluation eines solchen Systems nötig sind. Ein Nachteil bei der Benutzung von HMMs im Bereich der videobasierten Bewegungserkennung ist die Bedingung, dass für das Training solcher Modelle in der Regel viele Beispieldaten benötigt werden, die zudem idealerweise von Hand vorsegmentiert werden, um das Training kleinerer Bewegungseinheiten zu ermöglichen. Da die Segmentierung sehr arbeitsintensiv ist, gibt es allerdings nur wenige Datensammlungen, die solch eine Annotation in ausreichendem Maß zur Verfügung stellen. Daher wurden im Kontext der hier vorgestellten Arbeit zwei repräsentative Datensätze zur videobasierten Bewegungserkennung und -analyse erstellet und ein dritter Referenzdatensatz von Hand annotiert und im Hinblick auf die verschiedenen Aspekte der Sequenzerkennung ausgewertet. Diese umfangreiche Datensammlung bietet zum ersten Mal die Grundlage für eine semantische und syntaktische Auswertung von videobasierten Bewegungserkennungsverfahren.

Die vorliegende Arbeit evaluiert die vorgeschlagenen Flussmerkmale sowie das entsprechende System auf allen annotierten Datensätzen und vergleicht die Ergebnisse mit den entsprechenden aktuell besten alternativen Verfahren. Dazu werden verschiedene Qualitätskriterien betrachtet: zum einen die Erkennung der Gesamtaktivität innerhalb des Videoclips, zum zweiten die Erkennung der einzelnen Bewegungseinheiten innerhalb des Videos und zum dritten die Zerlegungsgenauigkeit, die die korrekte Erkennung der einzelnen Frames wiedergibt. Die Evaluation an Hand der drei vorgestellten Datensätze zeigt, dass das vorgeschlagene Verfahren in der Lage ist, menschliche Bewegungen in Videosequenzen mit einer bisher nicht erreichten Genauigkeit zu analysieren und zu zerlegen. Darüber hinaus erlaubt es eine bessere Erkennung, je komplexer die entsprechenden Aktivitäten werden und je mehr Trainingsdaten vorhanden sind.

Die vorliegende Arbeit beschreibt, wie Bewegungsinformation aus Videodaten genutzt werden können, um zugrundeliegenden Struktur menschlicher Bewegungen zu erkennen und zu analysieren. Sie zeigt damit einen möglichen Weg hin zu einer weitergehenden Erkennung menschlicher Bewegungen, die eine Abstraktion verschiedenen Bewegungskategorien jenseits der einfachen Klassifikation erlaubt.

Acknowledgment

This thesis summarizes the results of my research at the Institute for Algorithms and Cognitive Systems (as part of the Young Investigator Group Go.Human) and the Institute for Anthropomatics (Computer Vision for Human Computer Interaction Lab). The work was partly founded by the DFG Collaborative Research Center 588 - Humanoid Robots and the Department of Informatics of the Karlsruhe Institute of Technology. The Young Investigator Group Go.Human was supported by the grant from the Ministry of Science, Research and the Arts of Baden-Württemberg, Germany.

Karlsruhe, December 2013 *Hildegard Kühne*

Preface

Parts of this work have previously been published. The publications are listed in the following:

Chapter 2: H. Kuehne, H. Jhuang, E. Garrote, T. Poggio, and T. Serre, "HMDB: A large video database for human motion recognition", in Proc. of IEEE Conference on Computer Vision (ICCV), 2011.

H. Koehler, M. Pruzinec, T. Feldmann, and A. Woerner, "Automatic human model parametrization from 3d marker data for motion recognition", in Proc. of Conference in Central Europe on Computer Graphics, Visualization and Computer Vision (WSCG), 2008.

Chapter 3: D. Gehrig, H. Kuehne, A. Woerner, and T. Schultz, "Hmm-based human motion recognition with optical flow data", in Proc. of IEEE-RAS Conference on Humanoid Robots (Humanoids), 2009.

Chapter 4: H. Kuehne, D. Gehrig, T. Schultz, and R. Stiefelhagen, "On-line action recognition from sparse feature flow", in Proc. of International Conference on Computer Vision Theory and Applications (VISAPP), 2012.

P. Krauthausen, L. Rybok, U. D. Hanebeck, D. Gehrig, H. Kuehne, T. Schultz, R. Stiefelhagen, "Combined Intention, Activity, and Motion Recognition for a Humanoid Household Robot", in Proc. of IEEE-RSJ Conference on Intelligent Robots and Systems (IROS), 2011

Chapter 5: H. Kuehne, A. Arslan and T. Serre, "The Language of Actions: Recovering the Syntax and Semantics of Goal Directed Human Activities", in Proc. of Conference on Computer Vision and Pattern Recognition (CVPR), 2014.

Karlsruhe, December 2013

Hildegard Kühne
Karlsruher Institute of Technology (KIT)

Contents

1. Introduction

The analysis and recognition and of human actions in video data is a challenging task even for humans. As neuroscience shows [ZSS+07] humans perceive activities of their counter parts by first capturing simple body motions like hand or leg movements, followed by combining motions to simple actions or task executions and ending with the analysis of complex scenarios and activities as they are performed on work places, in sports or in the household domain. The recognition of human actions, as a result of this process, is needed in everyday life to interact with others, to learn new tasks, and to analyze situations that involve persons, from traffic scenes to movies and drama stage plays in theater. Thus it can be seen as an essential part of understanding the personal environment.

With the growing amount of video capturing devices arises the interest in automatizing those abilities. Examples for the need of an automatic recognition and parsing of human activities can be found in many areas of daily living:

- YouTube, currently the world's largest online video platform, grows by 100 hours of video[1] every minute at the moment. To get a rough idea of the significance of humans in videos, just counting the 20 most viewed clips at the moment[2], 17 clips out of 20 show human figures. Thus, information about human activities in videos can be an important cue for indexing and ranking on such platforms.

[1] `http://www.youtube.com/yt/press/statistics.html`, 01.02.2014
[2] `http://www.youtube.com/charts/videos_views?t=a`, 05.09.2012

- In 2009 the BBC made a request to local authorities in the UK to ask how many CCTV cameras they operate [BBC13]. As the report claims[3], Britain can be seen as one of the countries with the most public CCTV cameras surveying public places. For the city of London, which has the highest rate of cameras per person in Britain, an overall amount of 7413 cameras is reported. Considering the emerging amount of data in this field, it becomes clear that there is a need for an automated analysis.
- In the field of human computer interaction, the Microsoft Kinect™ interface, and earlier the Sony Playstation Move™ motion controller are two examples how the visual inspection of human motion can be used to interact intuitively with computer programs. One can assume that this kind of everyday life interaction with computers will become more and more natural as computers are becoming part of the daily life.

All those examples throw a light on the needs for automated processing of video data, especially with focus on human activities as it will be discussed in the following work. The following chapter gives a general overview of the topics and challenges of the here presented work. First, different applications scenarios in context of this work in which activity recognition can or will happen are described in Sec. 1.1. Related to the desired application scenario is the question of the granularity level that should be used to analyze and recognize human activities. Different levels of motion decomposition and concatenation are discussed in Sec. 1.2, also with focus on human perception as kind of existing gold standard. Based on those considerations, the contribution of the presented work as well as the related problems and challenges that have been addressed is described in Sec. 1.3. The chapter closes with an outline of the following work in Sec. 1.5.

[3] `http://news.bbc.co.uk/2/hi/uk_news/8159141.stm`

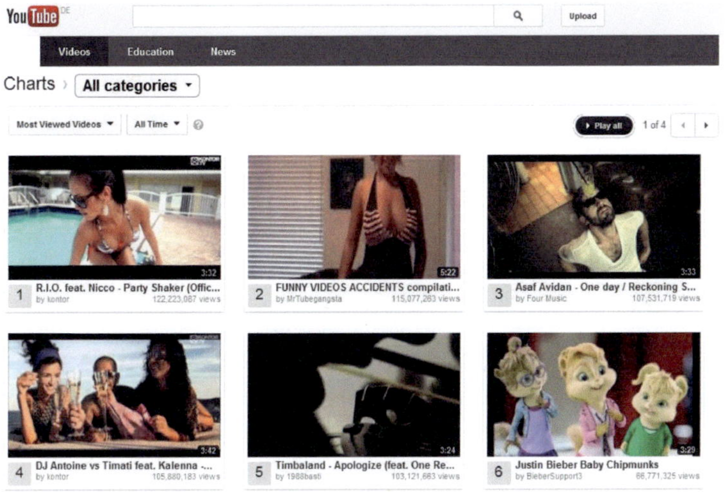

Figure 1.1.: YouTube charts for Germany, Sep. 2013. Five of the top six clips include human figures [You13].

1.1. Application Scenario

Some years ago, applications named in papers dealing with action recognition were rather unspecific like "surveillance", "human computer interaction" and "video indexing" [MHK06]. Over time, different and more precise problem statements arouse from those global scenarios. In the context of surveillance, the focus moved from simple action classification, e.g. to the exploration of concepts for unusual event detection [VA13, ZFFX11, ZSV04]. Likewise is human computer interaction usually focused on body pose reconstruction as the example of Microsoft Kinect™ [SFC⁺11] showed. This work focuses particularly on the recognition of structured human activities mainly in the context of kitchen and household. Some examples for the design of different kitchen scenes in the context is given in Fig. 1.2. Considering various benchmarks in action recognition published in the last years (see [MPK09, ITHM⁺13, RAAS12, TBB09, SKD⁺13, CSC⁺13]), this area is given considerable attention. It can be assumed that

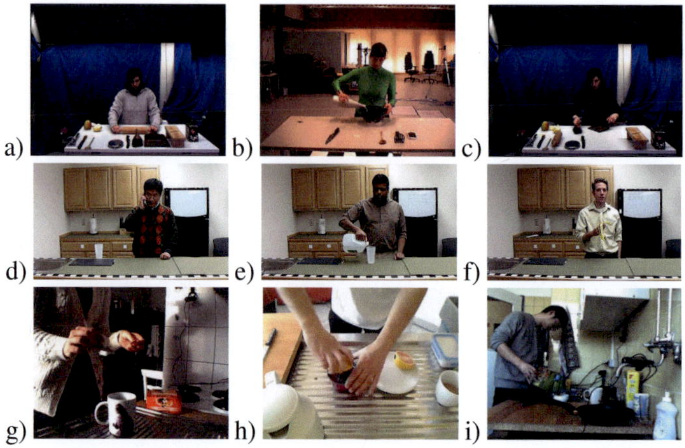

Figure 1.2.: Sample images from the evaluated datasets. From the BKT-Dataset a) rolling, b) pouring, c) sweeping, from the ADL-Dataset d) answer phone, e) drink water, f) eat banana, from the Breakfast dataset g) make tea h) make juice i) prepare cereals

the popularity of this specific scenario is based on different aspects: First, with the growing overaging of many western civilizations, there is also a growing need of ambulatory care to support elderly people to accomplish their daily life tasks such as cooking, cleaning or shopping. Depending on the level of care that is needed, all those tasks can require cost-intensive daily assistance. There are hopes that automated companions, for example in form of humanoid robots [ARA$^+$06] as shown in Fig. 1.3, could allow an optimal support of an autonomous life at an affordable price. In order to be able to build platforms that can interact with people in their environment and support everyday tasks, there is a need to understand and analyze the actions of the human counterpart. Second, considering the growing automation of daily life, there is also a trend towards a higher pervasion of the daily environment with assistive technologies, e.g. for smart homes or smart houses. In this case, it is requested that machines anticipate human needs a far as possible to reduce the interaction overhead to a minimum. Thus, the better the environment cooperates with its human owner, the less

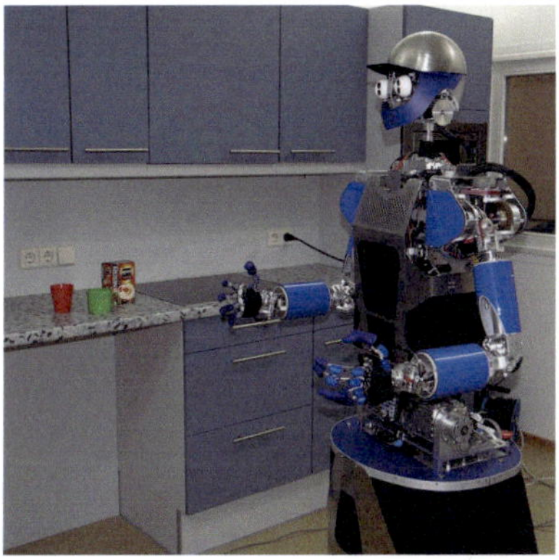

Figure 1.3.: Humanoid robot ARMAR-III, developed for applications in human-centered environments like service tasks in a household scenario (from [ARA$^+$06])

he has to care about it. Here, human motions and actions are a valuable cue to determine the following human actions and intentions.

Third, the various types of tasks as they arise in the household domain, e.g. in form of manipulation or modification of everyday objects, do easily transfer to a lot of other scenarios such as production lines in factories, cashiers in a supermarket or maintenance of complex systems like trains or airplanes. This generalization makes them an interesting benchmark scenario to assess and advance research in this field.

Finally, beside those various applications, there are also some practical reasons why household tasks are very popular in the field of action recognition.

First, activities in household domains are mainly task oriented. This makes it easy to define the beginning and end of a specific activity. They are usually self-contained activities. Second, tasks in the household domain are usually executable in a reasonable time allowing to record multiple samples even with limited work time and data storage. Third, there are no special skills needed to accomplish those tasks. This makes it easier to find test persons for a recording set as for example opposed to gymnastics or piano playing. On the recognition side, tasks in the household provide an interesting domain because they are usually more complex than simple locomotion actions like walking, but also well structured as they include a combination of actions that lead to a predefined result. They are usually independent of any cultural background and thus world wide understandable and can, with minor adaptions, be applied to any kitchen in the world.

The scenario gives also a good example of the requirements and constrains related to this application field. For all described scenarios, there are usually one or more camera streams available capturing the motion of interest. Therefore, the following work is based on 2D RGB image information only. Being aware of the fact that depth sensors are becoming more and more popular and that there can be more sensor input available, e.g. from gyroscopes, audio signals up to pressure measuring devices, it is assumed the vast amount of data in the field of human motion recognition is still based on single camera devices. Nevertheless, with a look to new upcoming benchmark datasets, one can see the importance of including depth information.

Another important aspect of generalization is to avoid assumptions about the current environment or objects involved. Considering the described scenarios, it is necessary to be able to work in known as well as unknown environments. Therefore the proposed algorithms work without any background knowledge, global or local environment models or the modeling of objects and their states. This does not minify the fact that the knowledge about further constrains can be helpful given the special conditions of a certain application. It is recognized that, e.g. object knowledge helps action recognition and vice versa [RSAHS14].

Opposed to the problem of combined recognition using different cues, the following work focuses on how far recognition can be realized considering human motion information only. The hope is that considering actions only for themselves in the first place also allows an improvement at more abstract levels and that this can be a valuable cue to develop better models of actions in context of their environment.

As the scenarios and sample data show, the work is limited to the recognition of only one person. It does not deny the need for a further recognition and modeling of interpersonal activities and dynamics, especially in the field of surveillance. But here single person action recognition will also help to improve models for complex human-human interactions on a higher level.

1.2. Granularity of Actions

In human action recognition the definition of an action is usually given by the label used in training. This works well for simple cases such as staged cyclic actions in a short video clip.

But the assumption of classifying actions by just labeling the whole video clip is hard to keep for action recognition 'in the wild'. First, there is to notice that people perform actions all the time. The production of actions is actually a continuous process. Sometimes this process is very structured and well defined, e.g. in sports, but it can also be some random unintended gesturing or the parallel execution of different tasks, e.g. in case of cooking or cleaning, where different tasks overlap or blend into each other.

The structuring or segmentation of human motions has been regarded by different research fields. Neuroscience research states that the problem of action recognition and understanding is closely related to the problem of action segmentation as discussed by Zacks et al. [ZSS+07]. Segmentation in this case is the ability to structure this input stream into meaningful parts.

This ability is actually seen as an important precondition for humans to be able to grasp an ongoing activity. Different models on human action segmentation have been proposed, e.g. by Baird and Baldwin [BB01] featuring a two-tier segmentation process. According to Zacks et al. [ZSS+07] the first low-level structuring happens on a fine granular muscular level, breaking motion into parts with constant motion direction. Then a coarser structuring which is comparable to task oriented segmentation divides the execution of one task from another. They point out that the segmentation based on motion changes has been studied over years, and people usually show high correlation on the boundaries defined by changes in simple motion properties like the perception of torque changes and minimums in endeffector position. The coarser segmentation is usually based on cues gained from the overall situation and therefore not as strongly correlated as segmentation on the finer level [ZKAM09]. They point out that the structuring process can be seen as part of the understanding and perception of human motion. The idea in this case is that people continuously make predictions about what will happen next and that event boundaries correspond to errors or uncertainties in the prediction process. Following [ZKAM09], it can be shown that the level of context usage also rises with the coarseness of the overall segmentation task. They claim that the structural model is essential for the recognition process because people use their knowledge about the temporal evolution of activities and anticipation of upcoming events as a mean to segment motion and to grasp and memorize the gist of an action. Those findings support the here presented idea of including temporal and semantic knowledge into the recognition process as well as the modeling of action recognition as a two tier process leading from fine granular motions to high level events.

Another discipline that is concerned with the literal representation of actions is the field of sports sciences. In sport science the goal is to define specific combinations of human movements, e.g. for the technical analysis of specific motions or to describe combinations of motion patterns for more complex tasks like high jumps or gymnastic courses up to complex scenarios like the strategic planning of soccer matches. On the level of technical analysis, the description can be very detailed down to measuring articulations in terms of changing forces on a force plate during a jump. On this fine granular level movements usually break up into a start or preparation

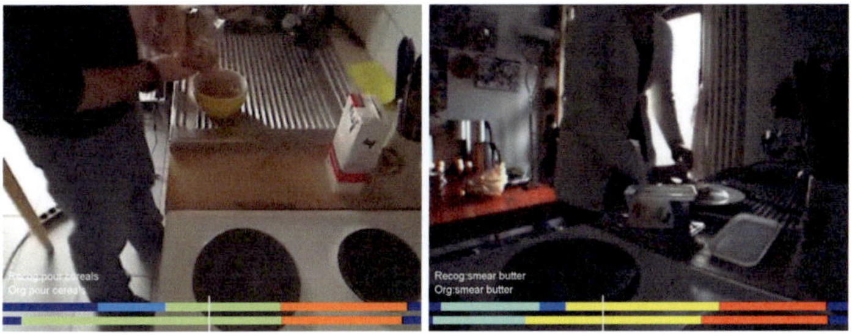

Figure 1.4.: Example for the recognition of action units for the activities “preparing cereals” and “preparing sandwich” from the Breakfast dataset.

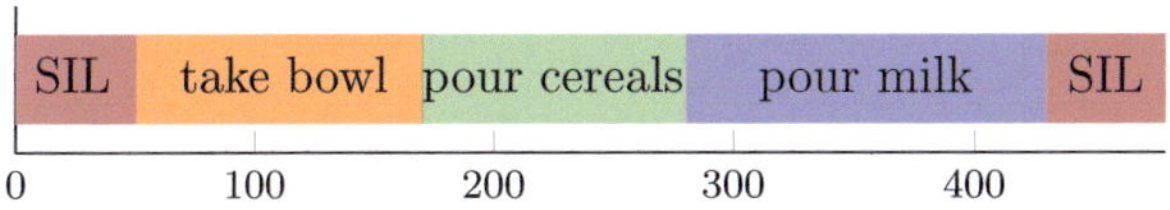

Figure 1.5.: Example for the frame based segmentation of the activity “preparing cereals”

phase, an execution phase and a finalization and adjustment phase including energy compensation or preparation of the next task. For higher level descriptions, for instance in case of gymnastic moves, the description is usually based on body configuration states leading from one position to the next. For complex sequences only a written choreography is used.

The here presented work takes up the idea that action recognition, and therefore also the description of ongoing actions, can not only be done by global labels, but can also be seen as a fine-to-coarse recognition process that includes multiple states building upon each other. An example for the segmentation of human activities is given in Fig. 1.5.

1.3. Contribution

The following work focuses on the role of action units and their composition in human action recognition, especially in the context of complex activities as they arise in the household domain.

In case of complex the videos involving different tasks one class label is usually not enough. Instead a combination of units over time leads to a sequence of elements that can be used to classify the overall activity but also to relate different activities among each other. For example "preparing coffee" and "preparing tea" are more closely related to each other than "preparing coffee" and "preparing a pancake". The notation of closely related can be expressed in the numbers of units they share.

This work deals with the question which techniques are appropriate for a recognition of units and their combinations. For this purpose action sequences are segmented into smaller action units describing the smallest undividable entity, which temporal position can change during the execution process [GKWS09], [KGSS12]. It is further assumed that the execution order is not random, but is defined by a set of rules that has to be followed to accomplish a meaningful tasks. Therefore, possible combinations of units are defined by a context-free grammar to guide the recognition process and to lead to the recognition of complex sequences. A context-free grammar is usually chosen in this context because it provide the strictest production rules to express a finite set of combinations of terminals [PR14]. Examples for the recognition of sequences of units are shown in Fig. 1.4.

For the recognition, an automatic speech recognition engine has been adapted to the purpose of action recognition. This allows beside action recognition the semantic parsing of the video as well as a frame based segmentation. As research in this field is mainly focused on the classification with discriminative classifiers, the popular high-dimensional space-time descriptors in combination with large codebooks [WUK^{+}09] seem inappropriate for the generative approach of a speech recognition engine.

To address this problem, features based on basic flow information are used to encode the video and generate an input that can be handled by this kind of system.

The performance of the proposed approach is evaluated on datasets with varying complexity dealing with the daily living activities like basic kitchen tasks or the preparation of breakfast items. All datasets are semantically labeled on a task level basis. An example for this frame based segmentation is shown in Fig. 1.5 and Fig. 1.4. This allows to build a recognition systems based on action units and grammar. It shows that with a growing structural complexity, temporal approaches are able to outperform discriminative state of the art methods. A simplified overview of the main evaluation results is given in Tab. 1.1 and Tab. 1.2, showing which combination of features and methods provides the best recognition performance for the three evaluated datasets. One can see that in case of frame based recognition of action units both the new feature descriptor and the proposed generative recognition technique clearly outperform present techniques. Only in case of recognizing the overall sequences correctly, the dataset with the fewest training samples is better classified with traditional methods. Here, datasets with sufficient training samples are usually better handled by the proposed method. Overall, the gain in accuracy for both cases shows that the strength of the proposed method lays in the frame based analysis of video sequences where the recognition accuracy is almost doubled compared to the reference method, rather than in the overall classification of sequences, where the gain is smaller or even negative compared to the reference sequence. Nevertheless the summary also shows that in case of the most challenging of the three datasets, the Breakfast dataset (BF), the proposed generative modeling can also lead to a significant improvement of the overall sequence accuracy.

Frame recognition accuracy						
	ADL		BKT		BF	
Features:	Prop.	Ref.	Prop.	Ref.	Prop.	Ref.
Prop. method	**52.3%**	45.6%	**91.8%**	82.1%	24.5%	**28.8%**
Ref. method	29.4%	21.7%	59.4%	54.0%	6.3%	6.4%

Table 1.1.: Comparison of best recognition performance of the proposed and the reference method and features for frame-based recognition of action units for all three dataset

Sequence recognition accuracy						
	ADL		BKT		BF	
Features:	Prop.	Ref.	Prop.	Ref.	Prop.	Ref.
Prop. method	76.0%	71.3%	**100.0%**	99.2%	28.6%	**40.5%**
Ref. method	76.0%	**86.6%**	96.8%	**100.0%**	26.0%	26.0%

Table 1.2.: Comparison of best overall sequence recognition performance of the proposed and the reference method and features

1.4. From Motion to Activities - Problems and Challenges

The problem of temporal modeling in context of action recognition has only been given few attention over the last years, e.g. compared to the amount of different feature descriptor variations that have been published.

To understand this lack of interest one has to remark that many developments over that last years are building up on findings in similar fields of research like object classification and are adapted to field of action recognition. To extend standard approaches as they have been used for label wise action classification to the problem of temporal analysis and recognition over time, different problems emerge on various levels.

The standard approach is usually built in three steps. The first step is the feature detection and descriptor computation. For detection, different methods based on local corner detection, e.g. Harris 3D [Lap05], Harris 2D [HS88] or Shi Tomasi [ST94] have been established. They lead to a number of interest points that are used to compute feature descriptors, e.g. HOGHOF [LMSR08], of their local surrounding. The output of this first step is a list of features descriptors with 72 up to 2000 dimensions, whereas the number of detected features varies from frame to frame, resp. from video to video. In the next step the varying number of features are summarized into a descriptor vector of fixed length. The bag-of-words method is the most common way to address this problem. Here, random features are sampled from the training data and clustered into 2000 up to 10000 clusters. The cluster centers are used to build a video representation. This is done by assigning each feature to its nearest cluster center. The final description of the video is the histogram over all feature assignments. The size of the video descriptor is based on the number of clusters. Current state of the art applications use vectors with 2000 to 10000 dimensions to describe a video. As a last step, the classification based on the extracted features is done by discriminative classification, e.g. by support vector machines or random forests.

Speech recognition engines are so far probably the most advanced tools in terms of analyzing temporal structures. They also fit well to the described problem of modeling actions as low level entities that can be concatenated to larger sequences. Additionally they allow a combined recognition and segmentation of temporal sequences. The final representation that is processed by speech recognition engines, usually in form of mel-frequency cepstral coefficients deviates from the input generated by action recognition approaches in form of video signatures.

Considering this layout of a speech engine, common approaches for action recognition do not easily transfer to the recognition and temporal analysis of automated speech recognition. The first problem arises on the level of feature detection. Assuming that a temporal recognition is based on recognizing or detecting small entities in form of action units over the video so that in the end, the result is similar to speech recognition: a representation of what happened when in the video. Units as small entities of action sequences can comprise 2-3 sec up to 10 to 30 sec (see Fig. 3.2, p. 46) resp. $\sim$50 to $\sim$100 frames on the lower end and $\sim$900 frames on the upper end assuming a frame rate of 20 to 30 fps. Assuming a mean distribution of 5 features per frame (see sec. 4.5.1, p. 81) a unit comprises 250 to 500 features. In a high dimensional histogram, e.g. with 2000 bins, this means less than one feature per bin.

When assuming a sliding window technique to generate a frame-based representation, there is a restriction in limiting the window size to the length of the elements that would be looked for. In terms sampling enough features, it is good to include as many frames as possible. But a too large sliding window results in an overlap of different classes. For the here presented case, a reasonable window size to choose probably starts at 20 frames up to 50. Assuming a detection rate of 5 features per frame, or 100 to 250 features per window, this would lead to sparse histograms, e.g. for the 2000 dimensions a maximum coverage of 12.5 % could theoretically be reached. Additionally, the sparse and high dimensional input vectors will lead to degenerated Gaussian mixtures as some distributions will have a very small or zeros variance in some dimensions.

Thus a better representation of frames has to be found. The here presented approach adapts well known approaches based on optical flow to generate frame representations that can be modeled by Gaussian mixtures and therefore serve as an input vector for an HMM based speech recognition system.

The proposed feature signature is based on a collection of flow features. The flow features were sampled over several frames using a relaxed threshold measurement to avoid unspecific background elements. By this, more features are found per image. The feature descriptor is further based on motion information by concatenating flow information over several frames. For the quantization again, a simple bag-of-words approach is applied, but in this case with best result found for a reduced cluster size of 30-100 dimensions. This leads to a low-dimensional dense representation of frames in a video that, as experiments show, allows a recognition rate that is either comparable or above state of the art.

The second problem of recognition and semantic parsing of activities over time arises from the lack of data to train such a system. Big efforts have been dedicated to the preparation and editing of speech data to be able to train complex systems. There is nothing comparable on the computer vision side. In case of speech recognition the Linguistic Data Consortium [Con13], an open consortium of universities, companies, and research laboratories, is among others one organization to organize the collection and distribution in the field of speech recognition. Their catalog comprised 715 different speech corpora from different fields like conversations, lexicons, and broadcasts in multiple languages. To get an idea of the size of the data corpora one can have a look at the most downloaded sets, which can be assumed to give an idea what is used in current speech recognition engines. The TIMIT Acoustic-Phonetic Continuous Speech Corpus [GLF$^+$93] comprises 6300 sentences overall, with 10 sentences spoken by 630 speakers with eight different dialects. Overall 2342 different sentences are included in the corpus. To get idea of the size, one sample sentence comprises 11 words and 39 phonemes. Also the design plays an important role for such datasets. For this datasets, tow dialect sentences have been designed as well as 450 phonetically-compact and 1890 phonetically-diverse sentences selected with the aim to get the best possible coverage of the dialectal variants of the speakers as well as possible pairs of phones[4]. Even for small corpora, like the TIDIGITS corpus for the design and evaluation of speaker-independent recognition of connected digit sequences, there are 326 speakers recorded each pronouncing 77 different digit sequences resulting in 253 digits and 176 digit transitions per speaker and ~8700 sample records. The data that is available to train one digit would correspond to 8700 instances of e.g. a waving gesture, recorded with 326 people in different contexts, and annotated down to the level of units. To compare this to existing datasets, the KTH dataset [SLC04] comprises 25 different people, performing six different activities in four different settings. Thus there are 100 instances

[4] `http://www.ldc.upenn.edu/Catalog/readme_files/timit.readme.html`

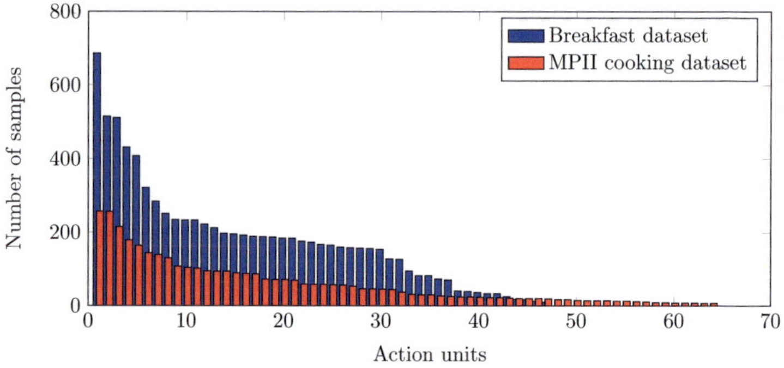

Figure 1.6.: Comparison of action unit instances for the breakfast dataset compared to the next larger MPII Cooking Activities dataset [RAAS12]

per action and there are no labels on the unit level available. The MPII Cooking Activities Dataset (MPII-CAD) [RAAS12] lists 44 videos recorded with 12 participants. Here the dataset is labeled, resulting in 64 different units with 7 to 258 instances and one silence class, but only few sequences are available for training and testing. To address this problem, two datasets have been designed, recorded, and annotated as part of the here presented work that allow for the first time to train and build action recognition systems comparable to speech recognition. Fig. 1.6 shows the comparison of instances for one of these datasets, the breakfast dataset, compared to the next larger MPII Cooking Activities Dataset [RAAS12]. Additionally, a third, free available dataset, the Activities of Daily Living dataset (ADL) [MPK09] comprising 5 different people, performing 10 activities three times each, has also been segmented and annotated on the basis of action units. Nevertheless it becomes clear that those attempts do by far not cover the whole spectrum of possible human actions, they can be seen as a first attempt for a proof-of-concept. Assuming that this proof-of-concept shows to be successful, it will be a further question, if more general models can somehow be defined, labeled and applied to a broader context of human actions.

1.5. Outline

The following text is structured as follows: Chapter 2 gives first an overview over current methods for action recognition in general and as well as for the special case of temporal modeling. Related to the here presented work, two datasets, the BKT and the Breakfast dataset, for the evaluation of complex human activities have been recorded and labeled. Additionally, a third dataset, the ADL dataset, has been labeled in terms of action units to allow for the evaluation of complex activities. The datasets and there related labeling and segmentation as discussed in Chapter 3.

Chapter 4 and Chapter 5 focus on the methodical aspects of the here presented work, describing first a new descriptor method based on optical flow information and designed for the recognition of action units over time and second the proposed approach for modeling activities over time based on techniques derived for automatic speech recognition, namely HMMs on the lowest level for the recognition of action units and actions grammars on the higher level to allow a concatenation of action units as well as a semantic parsing of the overall sequence.

Both chapters include the evaluation of the proposed approach based on the three described datasets. Additionally to the standard evaluation a set of new metrics is introduced to evaluate the performance of the sequential parsing of human activities. The different state of the art methods as well as the presented approach are tested and evaluated based on those criteria showing that the combination of proposed feature and method is able to outperform standard approaches under multiple aspects.

The work closes with a discussion of advantages and limitation of the proposed approach as well as with an outlook on possible future directions in Chapter 6.

2. Related Work

The recognition of human actions in video comprises different aspects such as person detection, tracking, pose estimation and the classification of human actions. Several surveys tried to capture the complexity of this area by finding different metrics and taxonomies to categorize the quantity of papers related to this area.

The overview presented in this chapter focuses on the special case of activity recognition comprising mainly approaches related to the recognition of action sequences such as larger entities with meaningful combinations of varying motion patterns. This can be seen as a special case in the field of action classification. It also means an important step from single action classification to a semantic understanding of ongoing tasks. Further, the increasing number of publications dealing with this problem shows the growing interested in this specific topic.

To give an overview of the various aspects of current research, surveys and their proposed taxonomies is discussed in Sec. 2.1. Different approaches for a flow based representation of human activities are listed in Sec. 2.2. Activities recognition approaches, those with a grammar-guided recognition as well as those without, are shown in Sec. 2.3. Additionally, the special case of action segmentation is considered. Sec. 2.4 provides an outlook to additional components that can be used for activity recognition. As research in the field of action recognition has also been driven by the available datasets, a review of the datasets related to the here presented problem statement is given in Sec. 2.5. The chapter closes with a conclusion in Sec. 2.6.

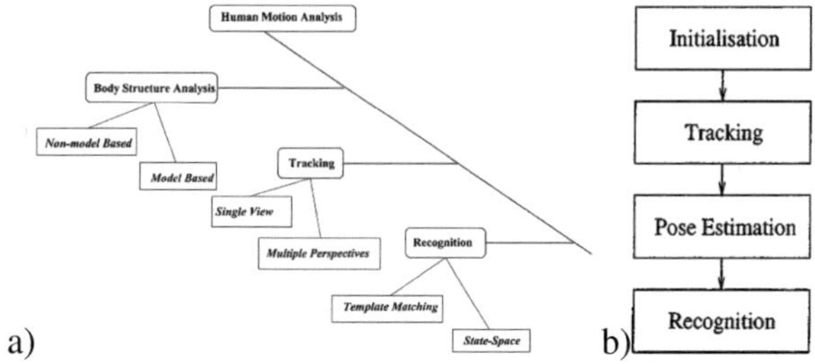

Figure 2.1.: a) Taxonomy for the categorization of human motion analysis publications given by Aggarwal and Chi [AC99] (1999) and flow diagram of a generic action recognition system presented by Moeslund and Granum [MG01] (2001)

2.1. Surveys and Taxonomies

One of the first surveys in context of human action recognition has been published 1999 by Aggarwal and Chi [AC99]. It focuses on human motion analysis, especially on the capturing of the human body motion, defining three major areas: body part analysis resp. pose estimation, person tracking and human action recognition from image sequences, as shown by the taxonomy tree in Fig. 2.1 a).

The following survey of Moeslund and Granum [MG01] from 2001 proposes a taxonomy based on the structure of a motion capture system, assuming that it will include persons detection, which is seen as the initialization step, person tracking, pose estimation, and the recognition of ongoing action as shown in Fig. 2.1 b). The follow-up survey of Moeslund et al. [MHK06] (2006) adopts this taxonomy. In current surveys those aspects are usually treated as separate problem and no longer mixed up. Instead surveys become more specialized and usually focus on one specific topic like person detection (Enzweiler et al. [EG09], 2009) or action recognition only (Poppe [Pop10], 2010). Turaga et al. [TCSU08] reviews the case of action recognition differentiating between two levels of complexity named as actions and activities, whereas actions refer to simple motion-patterns executed by a single human and activities refer to more complex and coordinated actions among humans. They emphasize that there is no strict rule

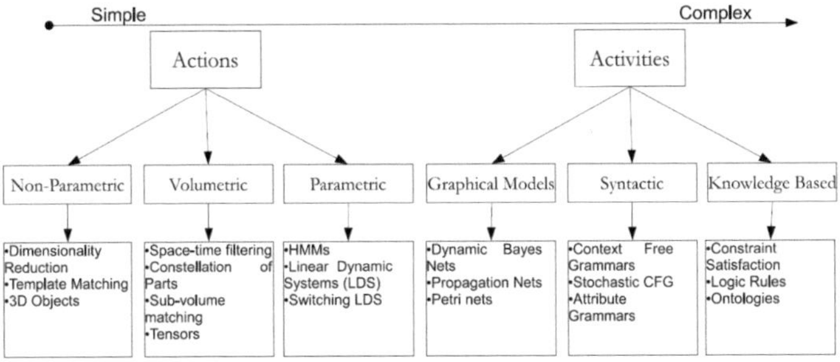

Figure 2.2.: Taxonomy for the categorization of human action recognition publications presented by Turaga et al. [TCSU08]

for the assignment of different action recognition approaches to one of the areas, but a smooth transition between simple and complex motion patterns. They give an overview for the proposed assignment shown in Fig. 2.2. The organization of the survey follows the processing chain of an action recognition system discussing the extraction of low-level features, design of action descriptions as well as their high-level semantic interpretation.

In [Pop10], Poppe (2010) defines the problem of human action recognition is as process of labeling image sequences with action labels. This can be seen as a condensing definition with regard to previous surveys. The survey comprises three main topics: an overview over common datasets used to benchmark action recognition approaches, image and video representation for action recognition as well as different classification techniques. Weinland et al. [WRB11] (2011) review the problem by analyzing different approaches to represent the spatial and temporal structure of actions, but also discuss the point of action segmentation in video streams as well as the problem of view-invariant representation of actions. They assume a generic action recognition system consisting of interacting stages: a feature extraction step, an action learning step, an action segmentation step, and an action classification step (see Fig. 2.3). The survey concludes with an overview over the most common benchmark datasets and the comparison of recognition accuracy of the different presented approaches.

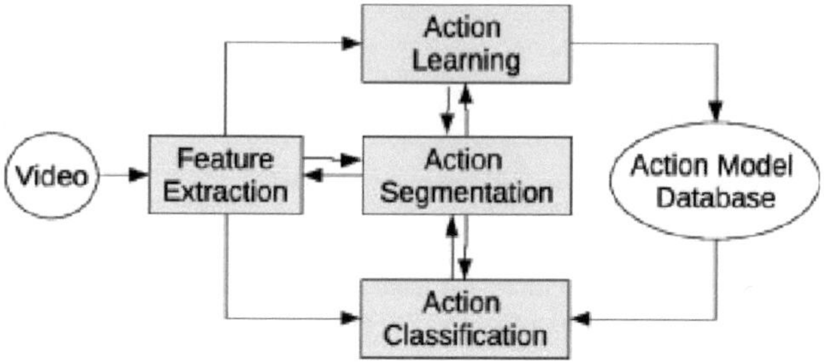

Figure 2.3.: Model of the components of an action recognition system proposed by Weinland et al. [WRB11]

A most recent survey by Chaquet et al. [CCFC13] (2013) gives an overview of the most important public datasets for video based action recognition. The overview lists an overall of 23 action recognition datasets and follows the level of complexity of the different datasets, ranging from simple periodic motions as shown in the Weizmann dataset [BGS$^+$05] or the KTH dataset [SLC04] up to multiview and interaction datasets as the UT interaction dataset [RA10] or the IXMAS dataset [WRB06]. The survey emphasizes the growing importance of benchmark datasets in the field of action recognition as they allow the fair comparison of recognition systems with the same input data.

2.2. Flow-based Features for Action Recognition

As recent surveys show, techniques to recognize human motion in a video range from local patches to image based representations and from descriptors based local gradient information up to the description of full silhouettes. As flow information is a natural way to represent motion information in a video, many descriptors that are related to the recognition of human actions in video contain flow based components to a certain extend even as they are not as popular as gradient based descriptors. The following section reviews approaches for action recognition systems based on flow information.

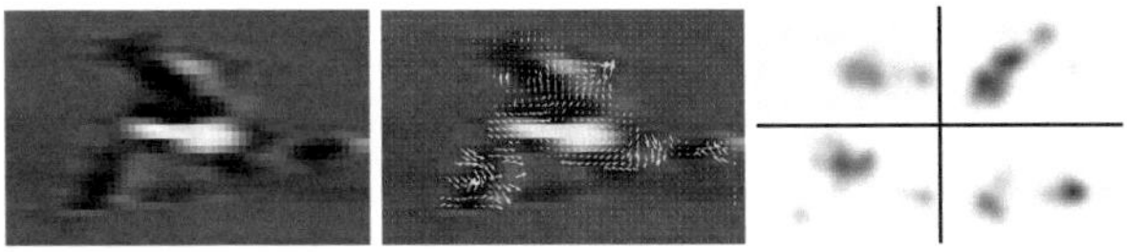

Figure 2.4.: Example of a flow based feature descriptor approach by Efros et al. [EBMM03]

As one of the earlier approaches Efros et al. [EBMM03] use Lukas-Kanade optical flow fields [LK81] to estimate the actions of players during a soccer match, a tennis match as well as ballet poses performed by male and female dancers. They first track each person within a suitable window. The final descriptor is built by splitting the tracked and aligned window into scalar fields for horizontal and vertical optical flow. The spatio-temporal motion descriptors are compared by of normalized correlation and to match the extracted motion descriptors with preclassified motions a k-nearest neighbor approach is used. Typical motions to recognize are for example running, walking as well as swinging in different directions for tennis and typical ballet moves like plié or relevé.

A more complex descriptor including flow information has been published by Laptev et al. [Lap05] (see Fig. 2.5). It combines the histogram-of-oriented gradients (HOG) approach [FR95] which is used for the detection of human figures in images in images [DT05] and recognition of objects [FGMR10] with a 3D flow based version of HOG, a histogram of oriented flow (HOF). This descriptor has been shown to achieve state-of-the-art performance on several commonly used action datasets as can be seen in [LMSR08], [WUK+09]. For classification, Laptev et al. use a bag-of-words system as described in [SLC04]. Based on Laptevs approach a lot of different local patch-based features have been proposed, e.g. HoG3D [KMS08], Sift 3D [SAS07] or Surf 3D [WTv08] which use combinations of gradient and flow information and accumulate them in a patch descriptor. Those features have the advantage, that the can capture a lot of variations of a representation. But to transform collections of those features into a video

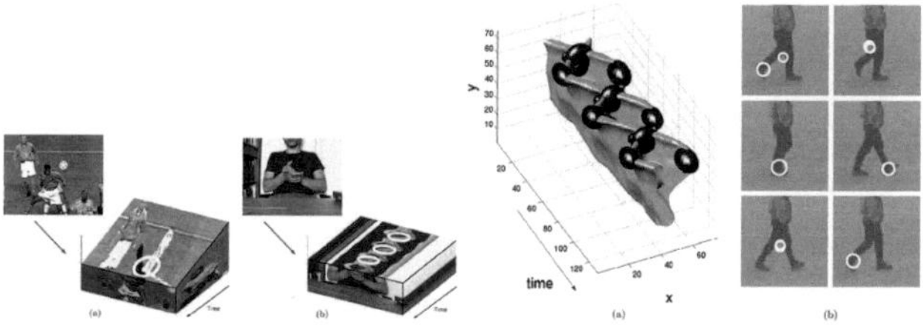

Figure 2.5.: Visualization of space-time interest points described by a HOGHOF approach as proposed by Laptev et al. [Lap05]

or frame representation by a bag-of-words approach, usually a vocabulary size of 2000 - 10000 cluster is used for an optimal result.

Beside the development of patch based features, different approaches have been proposed over the last years that are based on flow information only. A description of human activity in a video by motion information only is for instance given by Messing et al. [MPK09]. This approach uses tracks of KLT features [LK81] over 10 frames that are quantized by in log-polar coordinates with 8 bins for direction and 5 for magnitude. This form of quantization is in the paper referred to as velocity history. Additionally, they propose to add information as absolute position, appearance, color or the position non moving objects to the features to obtain augmented velocity histories. An example for the tracked features as well as for the codebook pixelmap can be seen in Fig. 2.6. The features are evaluated on the proposed Activities of Daily Living (ADL) dataset and provide a recognition accuracy of 63% for velocity histories and 89% for augmented velocity histories.

Another trajectory based descriptor, the so called trajectons, is proposed by Matikainen et al. [MHS09]. For this approach, a fix number of 100 KLT [LK81, ST94] features are continuously tracked in a video. The discrete derivatives of the trajectories over time, representing the motion over a fixed number of frames, are extended by concatenating them with an affine transformation matrix describing the motion of their surrounding neighbors. The final descriptor vector, called augmented affine trajecton, is a

Figure 2.6.: Example for tracked feature points and learned codebook pixel map for augmented velocity histories from [MPK09]

concatenation of the motion trajectory over a fixed number of frames and the elements of the affine transformation matrix describing the surrounding motion. The final representation of a video is the bag-of-words histogram over all features in the video. The method achieves comparable results to Laptev's HOGHOF features on the Hollywood Human Actions (HOHA) dataset [LMSR08]. Matikainen also proposes [MHS10] the augmentation of HOGHOF [Lap05] and the described trajectories by modeling pairwise relationships between quantized features. But the recognition accuracy of this approach with 70.0% on the ADL dataset [MPK09] and 59.0% on the UCF Youtube dataset [LLS09] does not reach comparable performance considering the accuracy of the original descriptors.

The traclet descriptor, proposed by Raptis and Soatto [RS10] combines KLT tracks as used by Messing et al. [MPK09] with averaged histograms of oriented gradients (AoG) and averaged histograms of oriented flow (AoF) that are extracted in the neighborhood of the tracked feature and concatenated into a traclet descriptor vector. As feature tracks are not limited to a fixed size but can vary in length, a dynamic time warping is used to allow comparability. The resulting descriptors are accumulated in a bag-of-words manner and a support vector machine is used for classification. As a different distance measure for AoG and AoF is used, the kernels are trained separately. The resulting approach reaches a recognition accuracy of 94.5% on the KTH dataset [SLC04] using a leave-one-person-out cross validation, and an accuracy of 82.7% on the ADL dataset [MPK09] without considering absolute positions of the traclets and 34.4% on the HOHA dataset [LMSR08]. [SLC04] and 89.7% on the UCF sports dataset [RAS08]. Shandong et al.

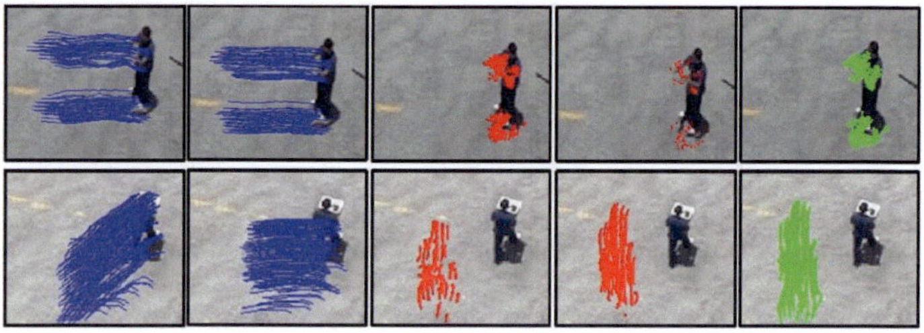

Figure 2.7.: Example for feature points and their motion decomposition as proposed by Shandong et al. [WOS11]

[WMS10] propose an optical flow based approach for anomaly detection in crowded scenes as well as for action recognition [WOS11]. They compute the optical flow for a complete clip and estimate current particle position by subpixel interpolation. The trajectories are clustered by their position information and the resulting scene is modeled by chaotic dynamics. Anomalies are detected by deviations from trained multi-variate Gaussian mixture models. In case of action recognition a rigid camera motion is assumed that is removed by estimating the global motion, and, additionally, the locomotion of the persons itself is treated separately from the articulated motion of limbs. They give a variety of examples for the motion decomposition as it is shown in Fig. 2.7. To recognize actions, the extracted trajectories are clustered into 100 cluster with the cluster centroid as representative trajectory and the chaotic invariant as described in [WMS10] is used to represent the final video. For classification, a support vector machine with RBF kernel is used. The presented approach reaches a recognition accuracy of 47.6% on the HOHA dataset [LMSR08] and 95.7% on the KTH dataset.

Another combination of motion information and local patch representations is presented by Wang et al. [WKSL11]. Here videos are also sampled by dense trajectories including optical flow information. For the computation of tracks, a grid based partition of the video frame is used and one trajectory for each track is built. The trajectories are tracked and sampled at multiple spatial scales treating each scale separately. Trajectories are additionally checked for heterogeneous image areas by using the eigenvalue of its auto correlation matrix. Regions that fall below a certain threshold are not considered. Similar to [RS10] a HOGHOF descriptor is computed along each trajectory. Additional features, called motion boundary histograms (MBH) are gained by quantizing the orientation information of the motion directions into an 8-bin histogram. A codebook of the size 4000 is computed for the trajectory, HOG, HOF and MBH descriptor separately. During clustering, K-means is initialized eight times and only the best result is reported. For the classification, the descriptors are combined in a multi channel approach using a support vector machine with χ^2-kernel. The results of this method are reported for the KTH dataset [SLC04] with 94.2%, the UCF Youtube dataset [LLS09] with 84.2%, the Hollywood2 dataset [MLS09] with 58.3%, and the UCF sports dataset [RAS08] with 88.2% accuracy.

Similar to the approach of [WOS11], Jain et al. [JJB13] propose a decompositional approach to capture actions in videos. They assume an affine motion model for camera and background motion and extract only the residual motion to compute local features. The feature descriptor is a combination of differential motion scalar quantities, divergence, curl, and shear features (DCS) [JJB13], computed from first order derivatives of the flow features. Further, they use a vector of locally aggregated descriptors (VLAD) [JDSP10] as descriptor encoding technique, which accumulates the differences of the vectors assigned to each visual word and characterizes the distribution of the vectors with respect to the cluster center. They report recognition accuracy on the Hollywood2 dataset [MLS09] with 62.5% accuracy, the HMDB51 [KJG+11] with 52.1% accuracy, and the Olympic sports dataset [NCFF10] with 83.2% accuracy. An overall summary is given in Fig. 2.1.

	KTH	UCF sports	HO-HA	ADL	UCF You-tube	HO-HA2	Olym-pic	HM-DB
HOGHOF [WUK+09]	91.8%	81.6%	-	-	-	47.4%	-	-
VH [MPK09]	-	-	-	63.0%	-	-	-	-
Trajectons [MHS09]	-	-	-	70.0%	59.0%	-	-	-
Traclets [RS10]	-	34.4%	82.7%	-	-	-	-	-
Particle trajectories [WOS11]	95.7%	89.7%	47.6%	-	-	-	-	-
Dense trajectories [WKSL11]	94.2%	88.2%	-	-	84.2%	58.3%	-	-
DCS [JJB13]	-	-	-	-	-	62.5%	83.2%	52.1%

Table 2.1.: Overview of flow based descriptors and their accuracy on different benchmark datasets

2.3. Activity Recognition

2.3.1. Activity Recognition Without Grammar

Over the last years, different approaches for the recognition of composed, non-granular activities have been presented.

Based on hand labeled trajectories, Rao et al. [RYS02] (2002) consider a temporal modeling by analyzing peaks and turning points of hand trajectories. They use the spatio-temporal curvature of a 2D trajectory to represent actions in terms of action units by dynamic instants and intervals. The trajectory is created from hand labeled instances which are inferred by a color based tracking approach. They model the temporal extend of an action based on motion trajectories composed of positions of the object for consecutive time instants and find motion boundaries by detecting discontinuities using curvature of trajectories and match representations with the equal number of instants and the same sign permutation. The representation is feasible for recognition and incremental learning of human actions and has been evaluated on a set of 47 clips showing different actions as "Open the cabinet" or "Erase the white board". In the evaluation, 21 of 47 actions are correctly matched.

Sminchisescu et al. [SKLM05a] propose an approach based on conditional random fields for the recognition of human motion. They mainly question the stringent independence assumption among observations used in Hidden Markov Models. Instead, they try to represent contextual dependencies by a flexible conditional model that is based on the previous state label as well as on the contextual window of several observations. They evaluate their framework with different input data: a vector of 56 3D joint angles that based on human motion capture and image silhouettes [SKLM05b]. Additional, they evaluate image descriptors based on silhouettes [SKLM05b] that are accumulated in a 50-dimensional histogram of shape context and pair-wise edge features at various scales. For evaluation, a fully ergodic HMM and a variety of CRFs are used. Given a realistic image sequence, they report a recognition accuracy of 82.2% for the CRFs whereas the evaluated HMM only reaches 68.3%.

Krüger et al. [Krü06, KG07] presented a HMM-based approach to recover the action primitives in longer actions. The inputs of their system are configurations of human body joints of one-arm movements captured by a FastTrack Motion capture device with four electromagnetic sensors. They define series of action primitives and model each primitive with an HMM with continuous Gaussian mixtures resulting in a set of HMMs, one for each action primitive. Additionally, an action factor is inserted as a random variable, which gives an estimation of the probability of a model of the observed action. The construct can be compared to a flat, one-state grammar. The reported recognition rates on a recorded test set are close to the general base-line of the HMMs considering identity and repetitive test cases.

Another approach based on video data is proposed by Niebels et al. [NCFF10]. They regard activities as temporal compositions of motion segments. They propose an approach to classify human activities by aggregating information from motion segments considering visual features as well as temporal composition. A video sequence is decomposed into temporal segments of variable length and each video segment is matched against one of the motion segment classifiers based on image similarities and the temporal location of the segment. Classification is based on the quality of matching between the motion segment classifiers and the temporal segments in the query sequence. The proposed concept can be compared to the concept of deformable part models in object detection [FMR08], but also relates to the field of action detection [GHS11].

Chen et al. [CA11] propose an action representation called *action spectogram*, inspired by the spectographic representation of a speech signal. They are using a bounding box around the figure and compute the related HOG and HOF descriptors. A low level classifier is trained on a grid basis and the output in form of calibrated likelihood values is used to synthesize the related action spectogram. For the recognition of composite activities, they use a hybrid HMM approach and generate the state probabilities on the basis of artificial neural networks and support vector machines.

Ryoo [Ryo11] exploits the advantage of temporal modeling for human activity prediction. In this approach, the problem of activity prediction instead of pure recognition is formulated as a probabilistic one and a dynamic bag-of-words approach is proposed to model the sequential properties of human motion. An activity is represented as an integral histogram of spatio-temporal features. The histogram representation of an activity model is computed by averaging the feature histograms of training samples for each time step while discarding all later observed features. The mapping of sequences is based on the likelihood between the activity model and the observed video and a dynamic programming strategy is applied to detect the activity in a video. The approach is evaluated on the UT-Interaction dataset [RA10] reporting a best recognition accuracy of 70.0% after half of the video is processed and 85.0% when the full video is used.

2.3.2. Grammar-based Action Recognition

As an extension of the temporal modeling process, a grammar allows the induction of semantic knowledge to the recognition process. This has two advantages. First it allows to guide the recognition process over time by defining possible combinations of states. This reduces the possibilities to parse in unknown sequences and thus helps to avoid of limit recognition. Second, the semantic labeling is a necessary condition to generate understandable, e.g. textual, information from an unknown video sequence.

The use of grammars in activity recognition, especially in case of a semantically meaning full representation, is still very limited, mainly due to the high work load that is needed to establish such a segmentation.

But various approaches have been made to describe human activities in grammar-like representations. A complete system for the modeling of human activities is proposed by Guerra-Filhoa et al. [GFFA05]. The presented human action language (HAL) is based on combinations of first and second derivatives of joint angle transitions. The resulting trajectories are encoded in rising and declining transitions, and local turning points like minima and maxima are used to describe the human motion. Guerra-Filhoa and Aloimonos [GFA12] extend the proposed human action language to the case of human interactions by extending their lexicon of human movement to human interactions such as shake hands or shove.

In the field of computer vision the usage of grammars for the evaluation of video sequences, especially in case of human motion, is still limited.

Ivanov and Bobick [IB00] used stochastic context free grammars (SCFG) to represent complex activities. The system follows a two-tier architecture with a lower level detection state to generate features candidates which are used as input stream for a stochastic context-free grammar parsing. The emphasize the advantage of using a grammar by providing longer range temporal constraints, disambiguation of uncertain low-level detection, and the inclusion of a priori knowledge about the structure of temporal events

They evaluate their approach on gesture recognition and video surveillance examples.

In [RA09], Ryoo And Aggarwal propose a context-free grammar (CFG) representation for composite activities to recognize two-person interactions such as "approach", "depart", "point", "shake hands", "hug", "punch", "kick", and "push". They define complex human activities based on simpler activities. Again, a two tier system is proposed. On the lower level poses are extracted based on the approach proposed by Park and Aggarwal [PA04] and gestures are recognized with pre-trained HMMs. Based on the recognition of gestures, the system hierarchically recognizes composite actions and interactions. They evaluate the proposed method on various surveillance videos captured by CCTV cameras.

Zhang et al. [ZTH11] propose a grammar-based approach for recognizing visual events. They use motion trajectories which are converted into motion patterns of moving object to represent the primitives in the grammar system. Additionally, a stochastic context-free grammar (SCFG) is extended with several logic rules to model relations between subevents. They use a multi-thread parsing and a Viterbi error measurement to analyze the given input stream. They evaluate their approach on gymnastic exercises, traffic light, and human interaction videos.

2.3.3. Action Segmentation

Closely related to the field of grammar based activity recognition is the area of action segmentation. As a grammar guided recognition includes an estimation of which action unit occurred at when in time, action segmentation approaches are mainly focused on finding the precise boundaries of action units.

A first base line for this task is proposed by Spriggs et al. [SDH09] by evaluating two activity categories of the CMU Multi-Modal Activity Database [lTHM+13] in terms of unsupervised temporal segmentation and supervised activity classification. As input, the video data of a head mounted camera and the sensor data of several inertial measurement units (IMUs) are used. For task classification, gist features at different scales are computed from the video data and concatenated to a 512 dimensional vector. The vector size is reduced by PCA and HMMs are learned for unsupervised task classification. Additionally, IMU data as well as multi-modal data is used for the temporal segmentation of activity into actions. Action segmentation and classification is evaluated on a frame based level and the best accuracy is reported for the multi-modal case with a K-nearest neighbor classifier reaching a performance of 57.8% for 29 actions categories.

Hoai et al. [HLD11] propose a joint segmentation and classification of human actions based on a discriminative temporal extension of the spatial bag-of-words model. They perform the classification within a multi-class SVM framework using the resulting weight vectors to infer over the recognized segments with dynamic programming strategy. After that, the weight vectors are used to segment unseen time series by finding the optimal segmentation that maximizes the difference between the SVM scores of the winning class and the next best alternative. The approach is evaluated on longer sequences of the honeybee dancing dataset [ORBD08, ORBD13], the Weizmann dataset [BGS$^+$05] and the Hollywood dataset [LMSR08]. In case of Weizmann and Hollywood dataset the sequences were created by concatenating single-action videos. The evaluation is done on a frame base level, associating each frame with a class label and reporting the overall accuracy per frame. The recognition rates reported are at 89.3% for the honeybee dancing dataset, 93.3% for the concatenated clips from the Weizmann dataset and 42.4% for four classes sampled from the Hollywood dataset.

Shao et al. [SJLZ12] propose a temporal action segmentation based on color intensity change and motion analysis. The approach is trained and evaluated on sport videos, trying to detect different exercise types and to count the related exercise cycles. The approach is based on first detecting the human figure with a standard HOG detector [DT05]. Then, a shape-based Pyramid Correlogram of Oriented Gradients (PCOG), calculated from the Motion Energy Images (MEI) and Motion History Images (MHI) as described by [BD01] is used to detect a motion cycle by applying a periodical action partitioning based on local maxima/minima detection. From the detected cycle, two key frames resp. their PCOG representation are sampled for the final action classification with a multi-class SVM classifier. The approach is evaluated on video sequences of eight indoor fitness exercises performed by 20 different subjects recorded at different scales and under varying viewpoints. Additional test sequences are sampled from the KTH dataset [SLC04] and from the Weizmann dataset [BGS$^+$05]. They compare their approach to a similar posed based approach proposed by Kellokumpu [KPH05] and report a best recognition accuracy of 98.0% for a pyramid kernel with three layers.

Zhou et al. [ZDH13] apply a bottom up strategy by using a temporal clustering at the lowest level to identify motion primitives leading to higher level representations, e.g. by applying dynamic time kernel alignment, an extension of dynamic time warping, to it. The proposed approach is called Hierarchical Aligned Cluster Analysis (HACA) and can be used for the unsupervised segmentation of multidimensional time series into disjoint segments. The approach is evaluated on three different data types: synthetic time series, motion capture, and video data. For video data the honeybee dancing dataset [ORBD08], the Weizmann dataset [BGS$^+$05] and the KTH dataset [SLC04] are used. For the Weizmann dataset, the silhouette and bounding box of test persons are computed and a maximum overlap measurement [CD00] is used for similarity measurement. For the KTH dataset, a velocity based descriptor similar to [EBMM03] is used, dividing the region of interest around the acting person into regular grids and computing local optical flow histograms for each grid. The final descriptor is the concatenation of all grid histograms and a χ^2-distance measure is used to find similar frames. They report a recognition accuracy of 77% on the

Weizmann dataset and 83% on the KTH dataset, evaluated on ten artificial testing videos sampled from the related datasets.

2.4. Modeling Actions in Context

As datasets become more complex there is also an increasing need to focus not only on the human motion itself, but to include context knowledge, e.g. in form of objects involved in certain activities such as playing a guitar or riding a horse.

One of the first attempts to include context knowledge into the recognition process was proposed by Marszalek et al. [MLS09]. They use a combination of action and scene classification to discover relevant scene classes and their correlation with human actions, e.g. the appearance of a car interior is related to the task of driving. To represent actions, a combination of 3D Harris corner detector and HOGHOF feature descriptor is used. For the scene representation, a 2D Harris corner detector is applied and SIFT features are extracted for the salient regions. Both visual models are represented within a bag-of-feature framework and combined by a joint scene-action SVM classifier. They show that the included context knowledge improves action recognition by $\sim$1% and that action knowledge also increases recognition rates of scene by $\sim$2%.

Another effort to include object knowledge into the action recognition process has been taken by Aksoy et al. [AAWD10]. In this case, the action-object relation is expressed by semantic scene graphs learned without any a priori knowledge. They follow the concept of object-action complexes by Krüger et al. [KGP$^+$11] describing the intertwining of objects and actions by which objects are represented by visual properties as well as by actions that are performed with it and actions are interlinked to their relevant objects. For the evaluation, elements on a table are segmented and tracked and a semantic scene graph is built from this information. The scene graph is adapted over time whereas discontinuities are handled as breaking

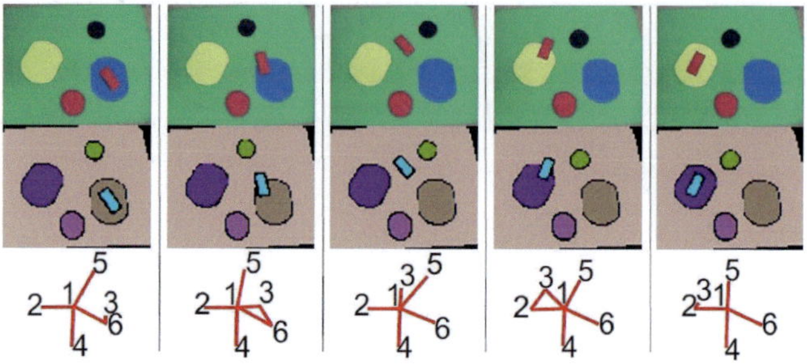

Figure 2.8.: Example for different version of moving an object as proposed by Aksoy [AAWD10], showing the original image in the first row, the segmented image in the second row and the semantic scene graphs in the last row

points within the sequences. An example for different scene graphs as they arise from object manipulation tasks is shown in Fig. 2.8. The concatenation of all scenes graphs is stored in an event table. The classification is done based on the similarity of different event tables.

Teo et al. [TYD$^+$12] propose similar to Marszalek [MLS09] the use of language as context for the recognition of action-object duality. But instead of using scripts, as done in [MLS09], which can be difficult to acquire, they train a language model based on the English news wire corpus to extract relationships between actions, objects, and spoken words in a scene. The proposed approach detects objects in a scene, extracts the verbs resp. actions related to this object from the audio stream, and confirm the predicted action with video based action features. They use an iterative EM algorithm to determine the optimal assignment of action labels to the videos with the highest probability. They tested their approach on the UMD sushi making dataset [Teo13], reporting a recognition accuracy of 91.7% for the semi-supervised EM training.

Koppula et al. [KS13] use an anticipatory temporal conditional random field (ATCRF) to model action object relations of the past, as well as to predict further motions in the future. They use a fully labeled dataset, including object affordance, activity and sub-activity labels, ground truth object categories, tracked object bounding boxes, and human skeleton representation to model the scene. Activities are represented by a hierarchical structure with an activity composed of a sequence of sub-activities. The interdependence of activities and objects and their affordances are modeled according to the relative position of the object. The trained ATCRFs are used to anticipate the motion trajectory of the objects and humans, and to estimate the planed activity. They report a macro precision rate of 80.6 % for past events and 37.9 % for anticipated events.

2.5. Action Recognition Datasets

During the last years, several datasets have been proposed that focus on household and kitchen area.

The most cited one is probably the University of Rochester Activities of daily living dataset (ADL) [MPK09] [1], providing 10 different activities such as "cutting fruits" or "answering a phone call", each executed tree times by five different test persons. The overall execution of the tasks is consistent among all test persons and varies only in detail, e.g. in the number of repetitions for cyclic motions or usage of left hand and right hand. All activities are recorded in a lab kitchen with a static, frontal camera and all tasks are executed at more or less the same position.

Another dataset is the CMU Multi-Modal Activity Database [lTHM+09, lTHM+13] (CMU MMAC). It comprises five activities recorded with different mocap techniques ranging from several cameras, including a head-mounted camera, gyroscopes as well as marker-based motion capture data. The tasks are executed by 39 different test persons leading to an overall of 870 samples. The multi-modal recording took place in a lab with constant environment, objects, clothes (marker suit) and camera position. That dataset is partly labeled. References and a baseline evaluation have been published by Spriggs et al. [SDH09]

[1] `http://www.cs.Rochester.edu/~rmessing/uradl/`

	ADL dataset [MPK09]	CMU MMAC database [ITHM+09]	MPII Cooking Activities dataset [RAAS12]	TUM Kitchen dataset [TBB09]	KSCGR dataset [SKD+13]	Opportunity dataset [CSC+13]
Persons	5	39	12	4	7	12
Duration	-	-	-	8h	-	-
Location	Lab	Lab	Lab	Lab	Lab	Lab
Cams	1	6 + sensors	1	4 + sensors	1 + depth	72 sensors
Clips	150	870	44	17	35	-
Activites	10	5	14	3	5	-
Units	53	29	65	8(10)	8	9
Labels	yes	part	yes	yes	yes	yes
Granularity	med	fine	fine	fine	med	fine
Extras	Feat.	-	Feat. + Pose	-	-	-

Table 2.2.: Overview of the scope of existing datasets considering data volume, recording modalities and annotations

The MPII Cooking Activities Dataset [RAAS12] comprises 14 activities which are fully labeled resulting in 65 different action unit classes. The tasks were recorded with 12 test persons using 4D Point Grey Grasshopper static camera in front of a lab kitchen. Additionally, annotations of the upper body position including shoulder, elbow, wrist and hands are provided for a subset of the dataset. The recognition is done for action units only, not for the overall activities themselves and focuses on the performance of holistic vs model-based approaches in this context [Roh13].

The TUM Kitchen datasets has been released in 2009 [TBB09] and is one of the first datasets that take place in a kitchen environment. Four different test persons perform basic tasks such as picking and placing objects or setting a table in different ways. Its main focus is the evaluation of markerless human motion capture and articulated pose estimation. Therefore, all activities are recorded by four cameras as well as with a marker-based motion capture system and other sensors. Labels are provided for each action [TBB13]. The dataset is mainly used for 3D pose estimation and motion segmentation, but also for action recognition from 3D pose information, e.g. by Gall et al. [GYG10].

Another kitchen related dataset emerging from the annual ChaLearn Gesture Challenge, the Kitchen Scene Context based Gesture Recognition Contest [SKD+13] (KSCGR) consist of seven persons, five for training, two for testing, cooking five different dishes ("ham and eggs", "omelet", "scrambled egg", "boiled egg", "Kinshi-tamago"). All actions are recorded by one frontal camera and one Kinect depth sensor. Both devices are placed above the kitchen table. The activities are fully labeled by eight different action labels such as "breaking", "mixing", "cutting" etc.

The Opportunity dataset [CSC+13] is a highly multi modal dataset, providing 12 test persons executing nine different activities such as preparing coffee or sandwich as well as a sample sequence in which different primitives were executed. The dataset is labeled on four different levels including activities and actions as well as locomotion, manipulative gestures etc. The activities are recorded by 72 different sensors, including camera [RCR+13]. The dataset is used to evaluate the influence of different sensor information in action recognition.

Other datasets that were related to action recognition but that do not take place in the kitchen but are still labeled, are e.g. provided by the annual ChaLearn Gesture Challenge, which was introduced in 2011/2012 and publishes various datasets for each challenge. The dataset for one-shot learning gesture challenge comprises 20 test persons executing 30 different gestures with one to five gestures per clip. Gestures can be elements of body language, sign language, pantomime, etc. The test persons were recorded by a frontal camera and a Kinect depth sensor, standing in front of a white wall. The focus of this dataset is directed towards one-shot learning by using only one example per class to classify the remaining gestures accordingly.

Finally, the POETICON dataset focuses on the recognition of interaction activities. It consists of six activities such as "cleaning", "preparing salad", "setting the table" etc. The activities were recorded with four pairs of actors, three times in a natural environment and three times in a sensor equipped environment. The test persons followed a scripted storyline

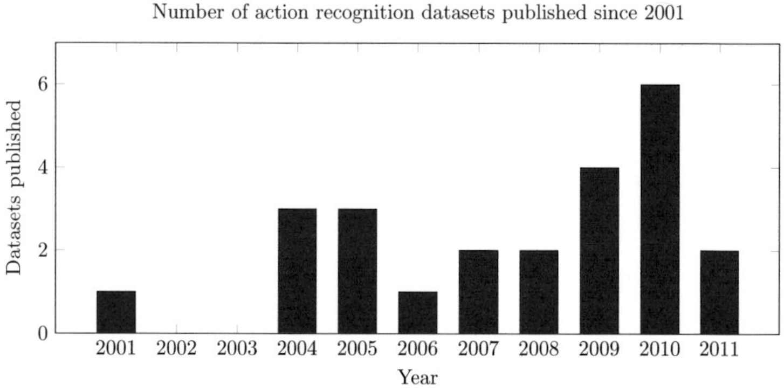

Figure 2.9.: Number of action recognition datasets published since 2001 (listing based on [CCFC13])

that they practiced before. In the natural setting five cameras were used, in the sensor equipped setting, two cameras as well a suit- and marker-based motion capture was used. Evaluation so far is only based on human perception of different tasks.

2.6. Conclusion

Overall, one can see from the trends in recognition as well as from the emerging benchmark datasets that the field of action recognition diversifies from simple action classification towards more application specific recognition techniques.

A hint for this is given by the growing number of emerging datasets. As one can see in Fig. 2.9, from 2001 to 2008 there were a maximum of three datasets published per year, whereas there were already 6 different datasets only published in 2010. As the complexity increases over time, there are also more datasets addressing specific scenarios in action recognition, as for example action recognition in unconstrained videos [LMSR08], but also interaction analysis [RA10] or multi-view action recognition [WRB06] and many more. This trend can also be seen by considering the topics of action recognition surveys over the last years. Whereas early surveys, such as Moeslund et al. [MG01], addresses the full spectrum of human figure related computer vision literature, newer surveys usually only focus on one specific aspect of this broad area, e.g. Poppe et al. [Pop10], Turaga et al. [TCSU08] or Chaquet et al. [CCFC13]. It can be assumed that this trend will lead to a stronger diversification of the field, trying to find different approaches to address the needs in specific fields and not one approach that works for all aspects of action recognition.

3. Datasets

3.1. Introduction

To evaluate the recognition as well as the analysis of complex human activities in video, benchmark datasets need to meet some prerequisites that can be seen as a foundation for the development as well as for the evaluation of such systems.

First, there is the need to comprise complex activities rather than short, single actions. Second, to allow a unit based training and evaluation, the related units need to be labeled. Those labels are difficult to acquire and, as seen in the previous Sec. 2.5, are only provided for a small number of clips. Finally, in case of generative models, the datasets need to provide enough samples for each activity, resp. for each action unit to allow the training of the related systems.

As those prerequisites are not met by any existing dataset so far, two new datasets, the Basic Kitchen Tasks Dataset (BKT) and the Breakfast Dataset, have been designed, recorded and segmented. Additionally, a public benchmark, the Activities of Daily Living (ADL) dataset has been segmented into units in order to apply the proposed algorithms.

The following chapter first discusses different criteria for the labeling and segmentation of human activities (Sec. 3.2). Then, the proposed datasets are described in detail, especially the recording setting, their statistical properties as well as their segmentation and grammar. Following the growing complexity the start is made by the BKT dataset (Sec. 3.3) followed by the ADL dataset (Sec. 3.4) up to the Breakfast dataset (Sec. 3.5) with the largest number of test persons and the most challenging recording setting. Sec. 3.6 concludes the chapter.

3.2. Dataset Segmentation and Labeling

The semantic understanding implies first a structural notion of the video content. This is usually done in a hierarchical way and follows the concept of language composition with atomic elements as a basis, called motion or action units or primitives, followed by one or more intermediate composition steps which finally lead to an overall activity description. An overview of different labeling strategies is given by Bobick and Krueger [BK11]. They propose two distinct criteria for labeling, a task based labeling and a motion based labeling. The task based labeling is guided by the state of the environment and its manipulation by the human, by moving or manipulating an object on the lowest level, up to complex changes, such as in [BK11], washing dishes, changing the state of the dishes from dirty to clean, or making a pancake by transforming different objects into something new. The task based labeling is driven by the manipulation process and starts, when the manipulation begins, resp. ends, when it is finished. The labeling based on body motion is focused on movements of the body only, considering motion direction changes or their first or second deviation as criteria of units on the finest level and composition of those elements on higher level semantics. This type of description for an action can be found in many different disciplines such as sports science, sign language or robotics.

Most datasets use a mixture of both aspects as labeling criteria, e.g. the Carnegie Mellon University Multimodal Activity database (CMU-MMAC) [lTHM+09] or the MPII Cooking Activities dataset [RAAS12], but it can also be seen that labeling tends to be rather task oriented than motion oriented.

Figure 3.1.: Sample images from the Basic Kitchen Task dataset

As the activities of the presented datasets are mainly based on the usage and manipulation of different items, the labeling used in this work is task oriented.

3.3. Basic Kitchen Tasks Dataset

The Basic Kitchen Tasks dataset (BKT) [GKWS09, KGSS12] has been recorded in context of the Collaborative Research Center (SFB) 588 - "Humanoid Robots - Learning and Cooperating Multimodal Robots" and features 10 different usages of kitchen tools. The activities are:

- Rolling (30 samples)
- Pouring (20 samples)
- Slicing (30 samples)
- Grinding (30 samples)
- Sweeping (30 samples)
- Grating (20 samples)
- Stirring (20 samples)
- Sawing (30 samples)
- Cutting (20 samples)
- Mashing (20 samples)

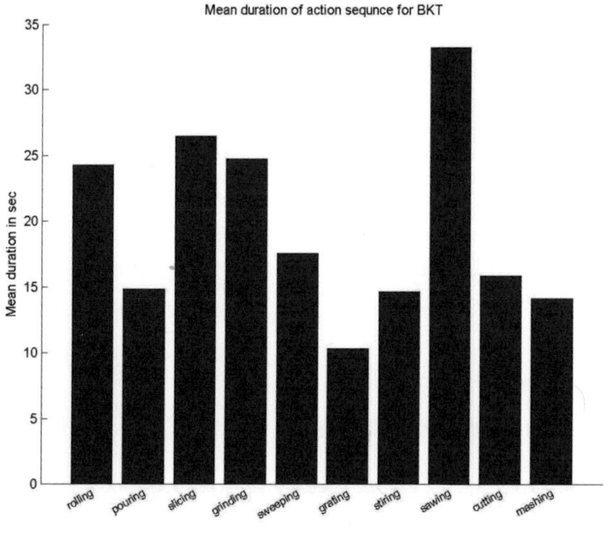

Figure 3.2.: Mean duration of activities of the BKT dataset in seconds

The activities rolling, slicing, grinding, sweeping and sawing have been recorded in a lab setting with a Prosilica GE680C camera with 25fps and a resolution of 640x480 px. The activities pouring, grating, stirring, cutting and mashing were recorded in the Biomotion lab at the Institute for Sport and Sport Science (IfSS)[1], KIT, Germany, with a Prosilica GE680C camera and two dragonfly cameras with 25 fps and a resolution of 640x480 px.

The dataset has an overall duration of 80 minutes and the mean duration per activity varies from 10 sec to 32 sec as can be seen in Fig. 3.2.

Additionally, five activities were recorded with a marker based motion capture system Vicon™ in order to compare video based results to a high-level system. For the marker based motion capture 35 markers were attached to predefined locations of the upper body [GKWS09] and 10 Vicon cameras

[1] http://www.sport.kit.edu/

were used. The markers were recorded with 100fps and the framerate was down sampled in a postprocessing step to 25fps. The 3D positions of the markers are used to estimate the related joint angle trajectories as input to a comparable motion recognition system. The marker positions were mapped to a predefined kinematic model of the upper body that has previously been adapted to the test persons anatomy. The related joint angles and positions were estimated by a nonlinear least square optimization [KPFW08] combining Levenberg-Marquart and Newton based gradient descend approaches [CL93], resulting in an 24 dimensional representation of joint angle trajectories for each frame. All tasks are executed by one test persons wearing different types of cloth. For evaluation, a 10-fold split is generated from the dataset.

All videos have been hand segmented by one annotator, resulting in 2407 unit samples with 46 different unit classes. An overview of the given activities and action units is given in Tab. 3.1. The distribution of units is shown in Fig. 3.3. As the recording of marker and video data was not synchronized, marker based joint angle trajectories have been segmented independently from the video data, using the same vocabulary and unit definitions. All activities consist of a preparation phase during that all tools are put in place, the execution of the desired task and a cleaning phase to put all used tools back and clear the working plate. As can be seen in Fig. 3.3 the units are equally distributed. Cyclic action units like "mashing" or "grating" appear more often than preparation or cleaning units.

3.4. Activities of Daily Living Dataset

The Activities of Daily Living dataset (ADL) has been published by the University of Rochester [MPK09] and comprises 10 different activities recorded in a lab kitchen with a counter facing the camera and kitchen devices and cupboards in the back. The activities are partly based on common kitchen tasks, but do also include other activities like making a phone

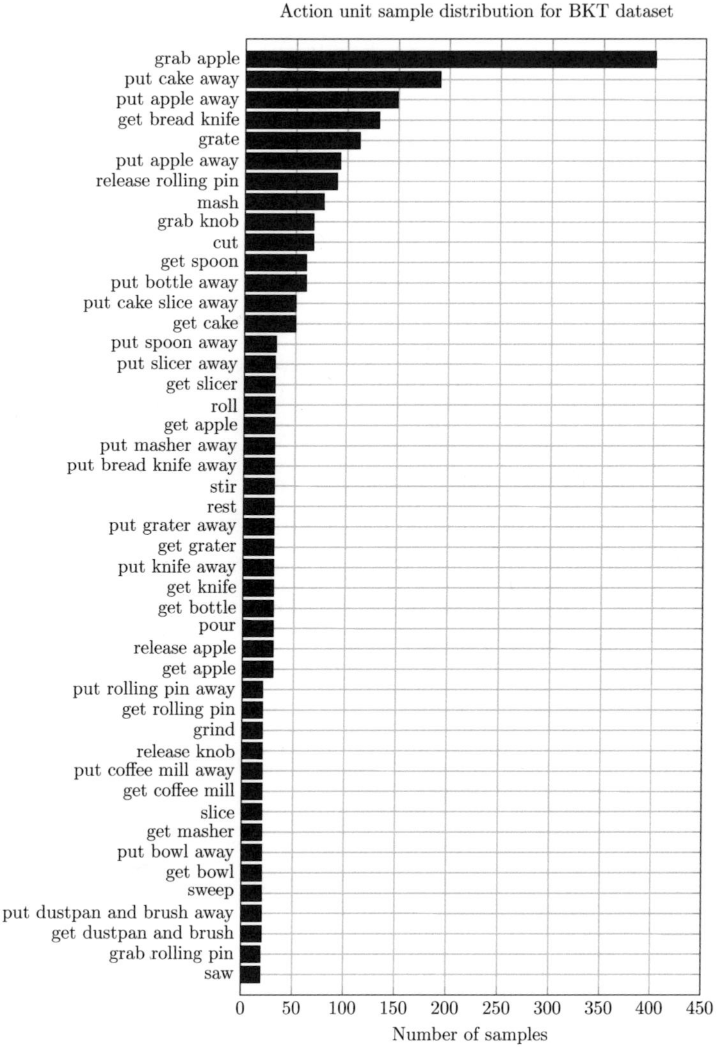

Figure 3.3.: Distribution of action units for the BKT dataset

Activities	Action units
Rolling	get rolling pin - grab rolling pin - roll - release rolling pin - put rolling pin away
Pouring	get bowl - get bottle - pour - put bottle away - put bowl away
Slicing	get slicer - get apple - slice - put apple away - put slicer away
Grinding	get coffee mill - grab knob - grind - release knob - put coffee mill away
Sweeping	get dustpan and brush - sweep - put dustpan and brush away
Grating	get grater - get apple - grate - put apple away - put grater away
Stirring	get bowl - get spoon - stir - put spoon away - put bowl away
Sawing	get cake - get bread knife - saw - put bread knife away - put cake away - put cake slice away
Cutting	get apple - get knife - grab apple - cut - release apple - put knife away - put apple away
Mashing	get bowl - get masher - mash - put masher away - put bowl away

Table 3.1.: Overview of actions and action units of the BKT dataset

Figure 3.4.: Sample images from the Activities of Daily Living dataset

call. An overview of all activities and the related number of samples is given in the following:

- answer phone (15 samples)
- chop banana (15 samples)
- dial phone (15 samples)
- drink water (15 samples)
- eat banana (15 samples)
- eat snack (15 samples)
- lookup in phone book (15 samples)
- peel banana (15 samples)
- use silverware (15 samples)
- write on whiteboard (15 samples)

All tasks are executed three times by five different people resulting in an overall of 150 clips. The evaluation of this dataset set is done by a leave-one-person-out strategy resulting in 5 splits, comprising each the recordings of one test person. Examples for the setting are given in Fig. 3.4.

One problem in the comparison of the presented approach to existing methods is the lack of segmented action data for training and evaluation. As no comparable datasets were available so far, the ADL dataset has been hand segmented into 53 different action units resulting in an overall amount of 1279 unit samples. For the segmentation, the videos clips have been equally divided between two annotators without double annotations. An overview of all units is given in Tab. 3.2 as well as an overview of the unit distribution in Fig. 3.5. One can see that, similar to the BKT dataset, cyclic and repetitive units like "chop" or "peel banana" appear more often than acyclic like "pour" and "pick glass".

Activities	Action units
answer phone	move hand to left - grab phone - open phone - move to ear - use phone
dial phone	move hand to left - grab phone - open phone - dial push button - move to ear - use phone
eat banana	move hand to left - move hand to right - move banana to mouth - move banana down - peel banana - peel banana
chop banana	move to back right - turn to front from right - arrange banana - chop - move hand to right - move hand to left
drink water	move to back left - open fridge - close fridge - turn to front from left - pick glass - move hand to right - move hand to left - pour - place bottle onto table - pick glass - change glass to other hand - move to mouth - drink - move hand from mouth
eat snack	move to back - open cupboard - close cupboard - turn to front - open snack box - move hand into snack box - move snack to mouth - move hand from mouth
lookup in phone book	move to back - open drawer - close drawer - turn to front - place book on table - open book - scroll pages to left - scroll pages to right - search entry
peel banana	move to back - turn to front - open banana - peel banana
use silverware	move to back - open microwave - close microwave - turn to front - pick up silverware - arrange silverware - cut - pick up food - move fork to mouth - move fork from mouth
write on whiteboard	move to back left - write on whiteboard - turn to front from left

Table 3.2.: Overview of actions and action units of the ADL dataset

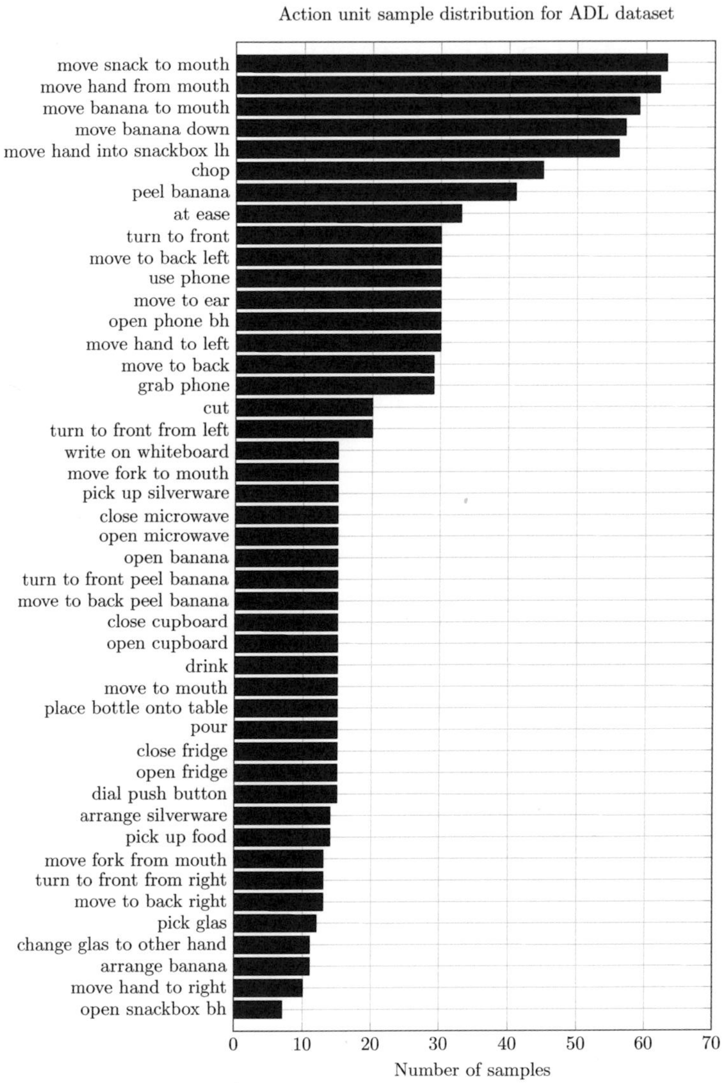

Figure 3.5.: Distribution of action units for the ADL dataset

Figure 3.6.: Sample images from the Breakfast dataset

3.5. Breakfast Dataset

The largest evaluated dataset is the Breakfast dataset. Until now, it can be seen as the largest fully labeled dataset available in this area. 10 different activities executed by 52 people were captured in 18 different kitchen locations. All activities were recorded by a set of three to five different cameras comprising two Prosilica GE680C camera with 25 fps and a resolution of 640x480 px, two Logitech QuickCam®Pro 9000 cameras with framerate of 15 fps and a resolution of 320x240 px and a Pointgrey Bumblebee™stereo camera with 20 fps and a resolution of 640x480 px. To capture a variety of different settings, the capturing took place at 18 different kitchens in apartments and university labs. In each location, the cameras have been placed at different positions in order to capture the working area and to adapt to the local conditions by kitchen layout and interior furnishings.

To reduce the variability introduced by different viewpoints, the dataset has been evaluated with original viewpoints as well as with unified viewpoints. As cameras have been placed in different positions and angles in each location, the viewpoint of each camera varies relative to the position of the test person. Especially views from the left and right side of the actor lead to different representations of ongoing actions, as the movement of a hand appears right-to-left in the camera standing on the right side of the person, and left-to-right in a camera standing on the left side of the test person. To unify the viewpoints, the location of each camera had been determined by hand. The videos, in which the acting person was recorded from the left side, have been mirrored so that, in the resulting video, the camera seems to be placed on the right side as well. In this mirrored version, all cameras appear on the same side of the actor, unifying the viewpoint as well as the ongoing motion directions.

The activities are executed by 52 test persons. Each person performs each activity not more than once. The activities are:

- Cereals (238 samples)
- Chocolate Milk (215 samples)
- Coffee (230 samples)
- Tea (242 samples)
- Orange Juice (215 samples)
- Sandwich (233 samples)
- Fruit Salad (227 samples)
- Pancake (212 samples)
- Fried Egg (228 samples)
- Scrambled Egg (220 samples)

To reduce the amount of data, all videos were down sampled to a resolution of 320x240 px and a framerate of 15 fps. To synchronize the clips and to avoid multiple labeling of the same activity, all videos have been jointly synchronized and labeled by hand. Additionally, they have been segmented at two different granularity levels, with the unit label as a coarser one and a second motion based label, leading to a fine granular description of the ongoing actions.

For the evaluation, four splits have been defined assigning 13 consecutive persons to a split. One has to remark that the recognition accuracy drops by choice of large splits compared to a full leave-one-out evaluations which would comprise 52 distinct test runs. The reduction in this case is owed to the runtime of the full leave-one-out evaluation compared to only four different splits as the reduced number of test runs allows a better comparability to other approaches, as it reduces the evaluation time to a reasonable quantity.

The dataset has been segmented into 11267 unit samples using 48 different action unit classes. An overview of the assignment of units to the different classes is given in Tab. 3.3. Additional to the relaxed environmental constrains, the activities here are intended to be less structured, e.g. compared to the BKT dataset, as one can see from the varying units. Whereas for many datasets, a more or less restricted sequence of execution is given, the test persons here were only ask to accomplish a certain task without further instructions, except that they were given a simple recipe from the preparation of a pan cake from the available ingredients. As a result of this relaxed setting, one can see that the activities have more variety and are more heterogeneous in terms of execution order. The presented dataset provides a labeling at two level of granularity: a fine granular level, based on motion changes of arms and hands and a coarser task-based unit labeling, based on atomic state manipulations like pouring milk. In this work, only the coarse labeling on unit level is considered. Additionally, one has to remark that the chosen activities show a high redundancy in terms of appearing action units. This allows the construction of unseen activities made up from actions units from already known activities.

Activities	Action units
Coffee	take cup - pour coffee - pour milk - pour sugar - spoon sugar - stir coffee
(Chocolate) Milk	take cup - spoon powder - pour powder - pour milk - stir milk
Juice	take squeezer - take glass - take plate - take knife - cut orange - squeeze orange - pour juice
Tea	take cup - add teabag - pour water - spoon sugar - pour sugar - stir tea
Cereals	take bowl - pour cereals - pour milk - stir cereals
Fried Egg	pour oil - butter pan - take eggs - crack eggs - fry eggs - take plate - add salt and pepper - flip eggs - serve eggs on plate
Pancakes	take bowl - crack eggs - spoon flour - pour milk - stir dough - pour oil - butter pan - pour dough on pan - fry pancake - take plate - serve pancake on plate
(Fruit) Salad	take plate - take knife - peel fruits - cut fruits - take bowl - transfer fruits to bowl - stir fruits
Sandwich	take plate - take knife - cut bun - take butter - smear butter - take topping - add topping - put bun together
Scrambled Egg	pour oil - butter pan - take bowl - take eggs - crack eggs - stir eggs - stirfry eggs - add salt and pepper - take plate - serve eggs on plate

Table 3.3.: Overview of actions and action units of the Breakfast dataset

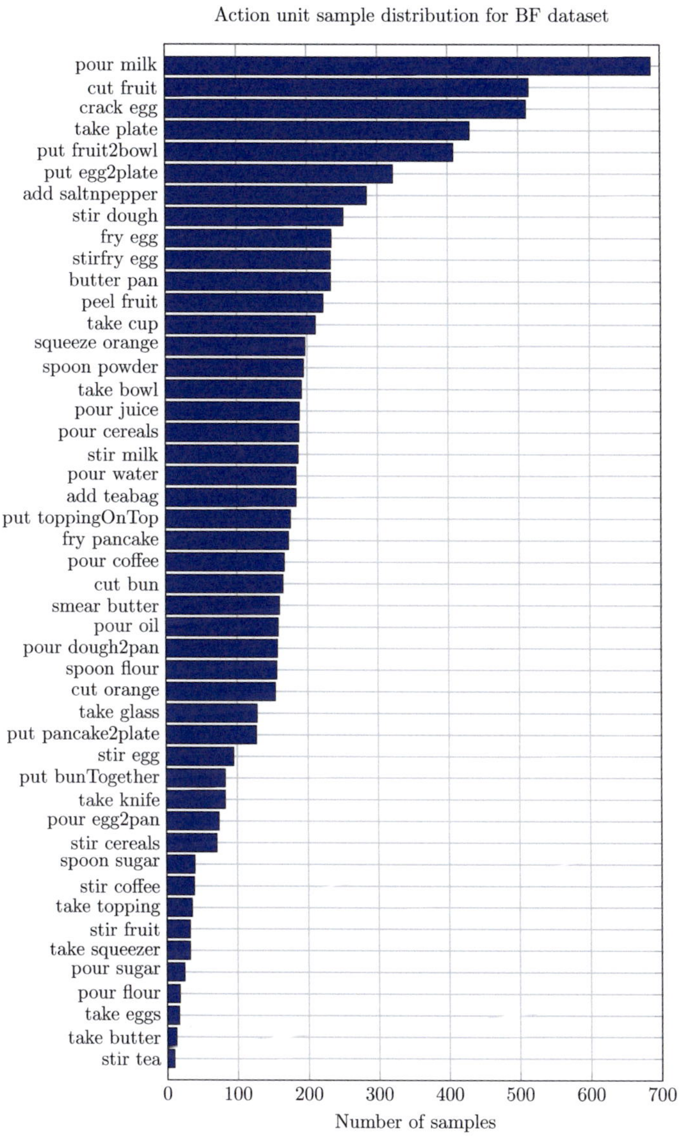

Figure 3.7.: Distribution of action units for the Breakfast dataset

	BKT	ADL	Breakfast
Subjects	1	5	52
Locations	2	1	18
Activities	10	10	10
Action units	46	51	48
Video clips	250	150	1721
unit samples	2346	1294	11267
Hours of video	83 min h	40 min	77 h (3 days)

Table 3.4.: Overview of general properties of the BKT dataset, the ADL dataset and the Breakfast dataset

3.6. Conclusion

The three proposed datasets provide a good basis for a thorough evaluation of recognition and analysis of human activities in videos. An overview of the scope of all three proposed datsets is shown in Tab. 3.4. Providing a growing complexity, they cover a broad range of evaluation criteria in terms of number of test persons, setups, complexity of the related activities and number of training samples. Additionally, all datasets are fully labeled, based on task-oriented criteria. Those accurate hand labels allow not only the training, but also the evaluation of sequential analysis of ongoing tasks. The combination of both elements allows a very detailed evaluation of algorithms for the temporal analysis of human activities in videos as it has not been possible before.

4. Flow Features

The basic task in order to classify videos based on the action is to capture the relevant information in the video stream. As raw pixel values are too unspecific, a higher level representation is needed. As seen in the previous chapter 2, there are many ways to capture the features relevant for the recognition of human motion. Flow information, as an intuitive representation ongoing motion, can be seen as one of the popular cues for this task.

The here proposed work investigates different feature representations based on flow information gained from the video stream. The processing chain is built as follows: first motion information based on optical flow is computed and concatenated over time resulting in a number of flow vectors for each frame. Flow features in regions with no significant motion a removed and only features in regions with significant motion are kept. The flow vectors of each frame are then aggregated into a histogram as the final frame representation. For the aggregation, different binning criteria from angle based to bag of words approaches are considered.

The following chapter describes the computation (Sec. 4.1), detection (Sec. 4.2), concatenation (Sec. 4.3) and quantization (Sec. 4.4) of flow based features showing different properties as well as the advantages and limitations of the proposed approach in context of exemplary evaluations. The overall performance of the proposed features is evaluated in Sec. 4.5. The chapter closes with a conclusion in Sec. 4.6.

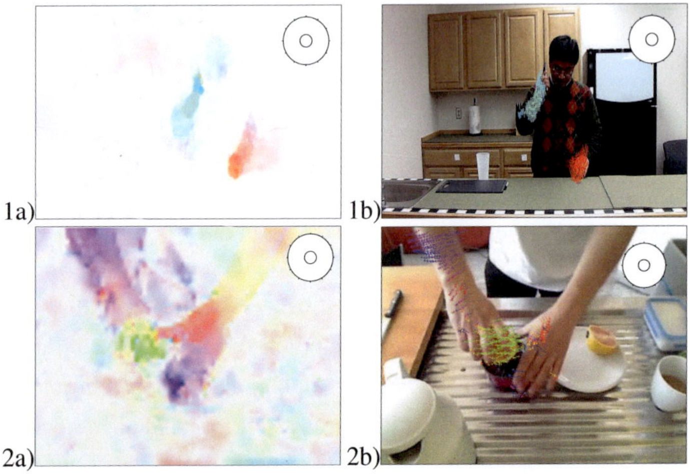

Figure 4.1.: Example for optical flow for 1a) and 1b) the action "answer phone" from the ADL dataset and 2a) and 2b) for "squeezing an orange" from the Breakfast dataset

4.1. Flow Computation

To compute the features, a dense optical flow based approach is considered resulting in one motion vector for each pixel. The optical flow is computed using the implementation of Chambolle and Pock [CP11] of a first-order primal-dual algorithm for the solution of convex optimization problems. In context of motion estimation, resp. for the computation of optical flow, this can be seen as a good solution as it models the non-smooth convex problem as a saddle point structure using a regularization term to handle the tradeoff between data fitting and preservation of edges.

For each pixel coordinate (x,y) in image I at time t the transition to the image at time step $t+\Delta t$ is approximated by the motion vector (u,v)

$$(x,y,t+\Delta t) \approx (x+u(x,y,t), y+v(x,y,t), t) \; . \tag{4.1}$$

As this work focuses on the processing of video data only, images correspond simply to frames of a video. In the following it is assumed that the motion estimation is always computed for a time step $\Delta t = 1$ without loss of generality. Some examples for the optical flow gained from different input videos are shown in Fig 4.1. The motion direction is represented by the color, and the length of the motion vector is indicated by the intensity.

4.2. Detection of Flow-based Features

In case of capturing human motions in a normal, natural environment, e.g. in a half or full body pose, only a part of the video is covered by the human figure and thus relevant for human action recognition. A simple example of the coverage of human figure and used tools is shown in Fig. 4.2. To estimate the coverage of human figure for the different datasets, a simple experiment has been conducted. For this experiment, sample frames of the proposed datasets have been labeled with the human figure including the tools involved in the current action shown by the red area in Fig. 4.2. Then the percentage of the labeled area is computed relative to the overall image size. For the BKT dataset the mean coverage over all labeled images is at 10.25%, for the ADL dataset at 17.53% and for the images of the breakfast dataset at 45.89%. Thus this experiment give only an approximate value, it shows that not all of the pixels of the video are relevant for the recognition of the ongoing action, and that the amount of relevant pixels can vary strongly from one dataset to another, depending on the camera position, the current task and the characteristics of the test persons figure.

To reduce the amount of processed data and to improve computation time and recognition accuracy, it is helpful to discard features from regions that do not contain valuable information. Different strategies to choose regions to compute features from have been taken into consideration. The detection techniques need to result in a good quantitative representation of the ongoing flow, and, additionally, would provide enough feature points to build

a)
b)
c)

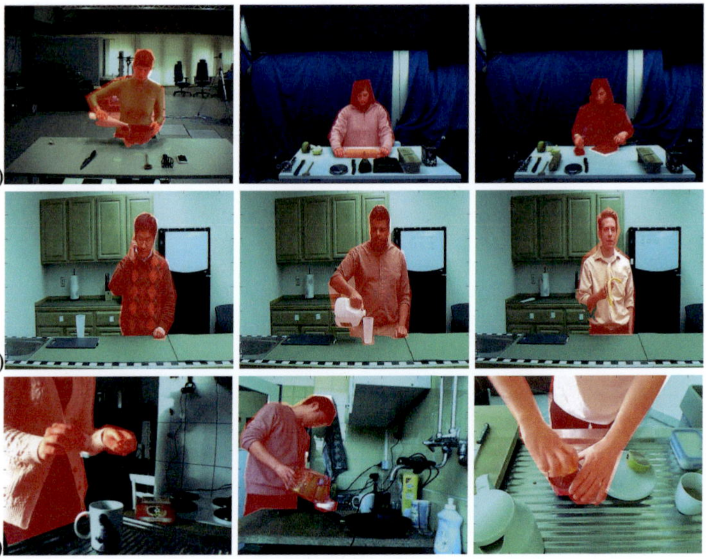

Figure 4.2.: Coverage of human figure in the image area evaluated for some sample frames of the BKT dataset (a) with a mean coverage of 10.25%, the ADL dataset (b) with a mean coverage of 17.53% and the Breakfast dataset (c) with a mean coverage of 45.89%

dense histograms over short periods of time, for example a sliding window of 5 to 20 frames. Therefore, corner-based methods, which have shown good results, e.g. for [Lap05], but result only in sparse feature point sets have not been considered. Instead, the focus for the detection of relevant feature sets lays on region based methods, especially based on intensity differences and flow volumes.

4.2.1. Frame-difference based Detection

In terms of motion-based feature detection one method is to define regions with intensity changes as an indication for ongoing motion. To do this, the difference image I_{diff} of two or more temporally adjacent frames I_t and

$I_{t+\Delta t}$ is described by

$$I_{diff} = \sqrt{(I_{t+\Delta t} - I_t)^2} \,. \tag{4.2}$$

The difference image I_{diff} can be binarized by a static threshold to obtain a first approximation for a mask image I_{mask}, which will define the region-of-interest in which existing features are tracked. Because of small motion variations from one frame to the next one, a low fixed threshold depending on the mean intensity μ_i of the difference image I_{diff} can be applied to the difference image I_{diff} to generate the mask image I_{mask}:

$$I_{mask}(x,y) = \begin{cases} 1, & I_{diff}(x,y) \leq a\mu_i, \\ 0, & I_{diff}(x,y) > a\mu_i, \end{cases} \tag{4.3}$$

where

$$\mu_i = \frac{1}{nm} \sum_{x=1}^{n} \sum_{y=1}^{m} I_{diff}(x,y) \,, \tag{4.4}$$

with n, m corresponding to width and height of I_{diff} and a corresponding to the scaling factor.

An example for the results gained with frame based differences is shown in Fig. 4.3 based on the sample image shown in Fig. 4.1 where a) shows the simple difference over two frames, b) the mask image resulting from simple threshold operation, and c) the mask image after morphological opening and closing with a smaller and larger structuring element. One can see that some noise could be removed, but still larger areas of the body are not covered due to color constancy.

To evaluate this method, the resulting area is compared to the labeled area of several frames. Fig. 4.4 shows an example for the coverage of the complete body. To enlarge the covered space, the difference of a) one, b) three and c) five frames has been considered. The figure shows a comparison of the detected regions with respect to the labeled ground truth. The correctly labeled pixels are shown in red, the false negatives are shown in

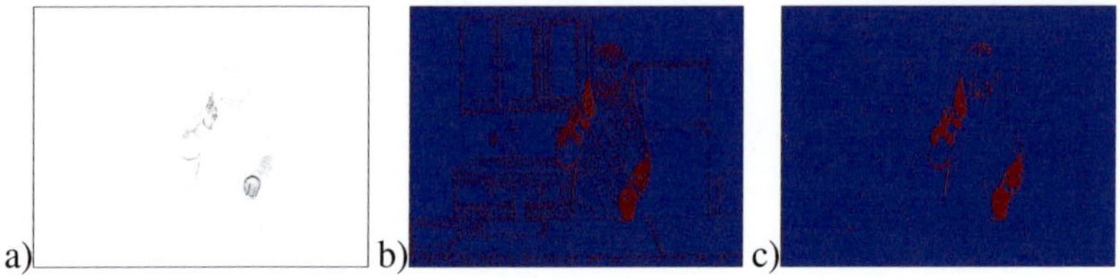

Figure 4.3.: Example for frame based differences showing a) the simple (inverted) difference between two frames with darker values indicating larger differences, b) the simple threshold mask and c) the mask image after morphological post processing

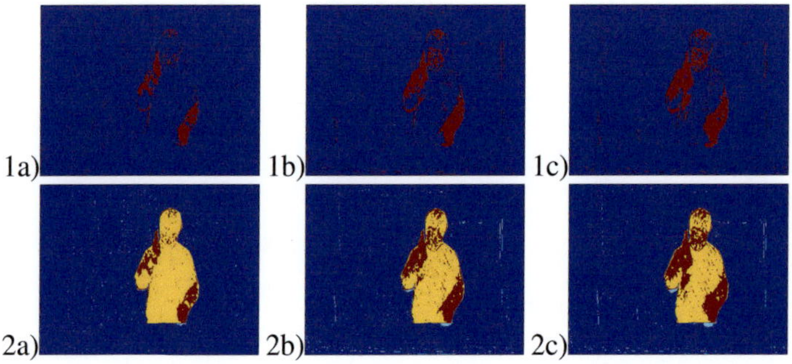

Figure 4.4.: Comparison of frame differences (1) with the labeled ground truth (2) showing results for a) one frame, b) three frames and c) five frames. False positives are marked in cyan and false negatives are shown in yellow.

yellow, the false positives are marked in cyan and the true negative pixels are shown in blue. The amount of falsely classified pixels with respect to the original label is 83.87% for the difference of one frame to another, 73.71% for the difference over three frames and 65.39% for the difference over five frames.

4.2.2. Flow-based Detection

Another way is to define the related region of interest based on the aggregation of flow information. In this case, not the difference of image values, but the previously computed optical flow of each frame is considered. The motion energy is defined as

To omit areas without significant motion information the lower bound for the minimal motion energy is depending on the the maximum flow energy of the two motion vectors:

$$e = \max_{x,y,t}\{u(x,y,t), v(x,y,t)\} \; . \tag{4.5}$$

The threshold for the intensity level extracted from the cumulative histogram C given by

$$C_e = \sum_{j=1}^{i} n_j \; . \tag{4.6}$$

C_e denotes the i-th bin of the cumulative histogram over the bins h_j defined by

$$n = \sum_{i=1}^{k} h_i \; , \tag{4.7}$$

where n is the number of all flow features and k the number of elements of the related bins. The threshold is defined by omitting 90% - 95% of the cumulative histogram. An example of the resulting regions is shown in Fig. 4.5

The threshold is computed for each video independently. For the evaluation, the threshold factor has been adapted to each dataset individually.

The choice of a fixed threshold per video is based on two assumptions. As shown in Fig. 4.2, usually different types of action are recorded within one dataset. One can assume that the relevant part of vectors might be small, but with a highly heterogeneous motion energy. Thus, adaptive methods that minimize the inter class variance, e.g. Otzus method [Ots79], might lead to an under segmentation, and hence, leave out valid areas with small motion energy. Additionally, videos of a dataset might have varying distributions in terms of minimal motion energy, because of different

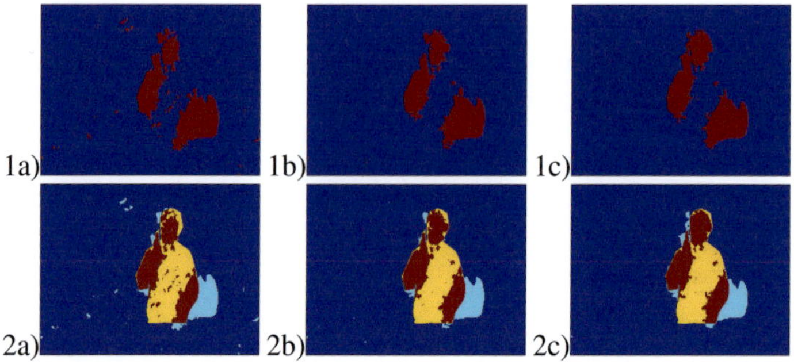

Figure 4.5.: Example for flow-based feature detection showing results for a) one frame, b) three frames and c) five frames as well as the comparison with the outlined human figure for the action 'answer phone'.

action types, test persons activity execution, etc. In this case, a fix threshold produces better results by keeping the overall amount of extracted features more stable, comparable, and person and activity independent than adaptive methods.

4.2.3. Comparison with Dense Sampling

Another popular strategy, for example used by [WUK$^+$09], is dense sampling. Here the video is divided into regular blocks and features are computed for each block. This leads to a high amount of features as well as a constant number of features per frame for a fixed video resolution. Dense sampling has the advantage that no information is lost in the preprocessing, but it also results in more data than detection based methods.

For the evaluation of the two feature selection techniques and for the comparison with dense sampling, a set of sample frames has been annotated, providing the contour of the test person and the objects involved in the current action. It is assumed that the annotated areas corresponds to the pixels of interest for the recognition of the ongoing action. The area is compared to the results of frame based differences as well as to the results of flow based detection. Tab. 4.1 shows the precision, recall, and F-score

	Frame diff	Flow detect	Dense
Precision	89.59%	79.51%	24.25%
Recall	14.63%	57.09%	100.0%
F-score	24.36%	**63.48%**	37.76%

Table 4.1.: Comparison of detection accuracy for frame based and flow based detection

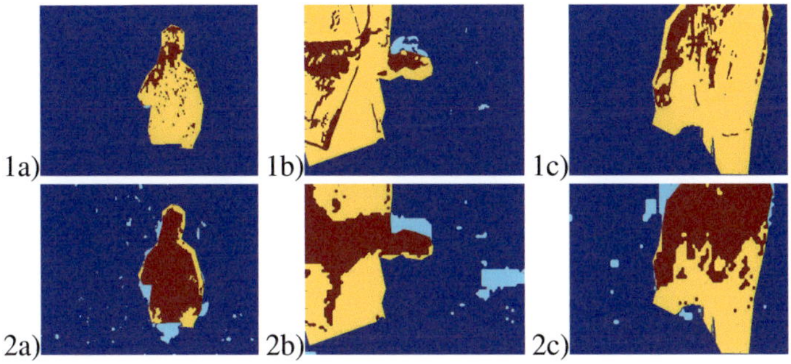

Figure 4.6.: Example for (1) frame based and (2) flow based detection of features for three different frames (a-c). Flow based detection provides a better coverage of the labeled area.

measurement for the different methods. One can see that frame-based difference reaches a high precision, but a low recall, because the boundaries of the person and moving objects are well defined, but the area of the body is usually lost due to color and intensity constancy, as can be seen in Fig. 4.6. The opposite case holds for dense sampling where the recall is naturally 100%, but the precision is very low and corresponds to the amount of labeled pixels. Looking at the F-score, the proposed flow-based difference measurement shows best the trade-off between precision and recall of the detected area. As can be seen from the examples in Fig. 4.6, flow based detection usually allows the detection of all moving body parts and objects in the image and provides a better coverage of the labeled area compared to the other evaluated methods.

4.3. Flow Vector Concatenation

As optical flow represents a mapping from one frame to the next and does not involve longer temporal representations, the extension of motion vectors over multiple frames is needed. Therefore optical flow vectors are concatenated, using the endpoint of the motion vector as start point for the following vector. The result is a motion vector over multiple frames, which is call a called flow feature. A flow feature v is defined as vector of continuous motion shifts over f frames by

$$v = (u_1, \dots, u_f, v_1, \dots, v_f) \,. \tag{4.8}$$

Here, the assumption of discrete positions in case of optical flow is not sufficient. As optical flow is continuous, following the motion vector from one frame to the next and concatenating it with the motion vector of the resulting frame would lead to a round-off error, depending on the approximation needed. Considering the concatenation over several frames this leads to an accumulating error over time.

To avoid this, the following work proposes a weighted subpixel interpolation over the optical flow of adjacent pixels to generate the new motion vector. Each concatenated vector starts at a discrete position (x,y,t). Adding up the related motion shift results in the position $x+u(x,y,t), y+v(x,y,t)$ for the next frame $t+1$. The following motion vector is computed by a weighted combination of the neighboring motion vectors at each time step, considering a four by four neighborhood. The neighborhood is defined by the coordinates $(a,b,t+1)$, $(a+1,b,t+1)$, $(a,b+1,t+1)$ and $(a+1,b+1,t+1)$ with $a < x+u(x,y,t) < a+1$ and $b < y+v(x,y,t) < b+1$ as can be seen in Fig. 4.7. The distance of a and $x+u(x,y,t)$ is called α_x and of b and $y+v(x,y,t)$ is α_y. To compute the motion vector (u,v) at the position $(x+u(x,y,t), y+v(x,y,t), t+1)$, bilinear interpolation [ZF03] is used. It is

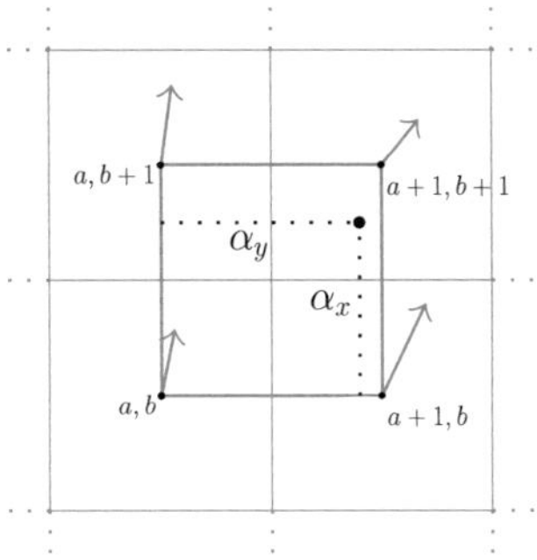

Figure 4.7.: Schematic overview of computation of interpolated motion vector $(u(a+\alpha_x, b+\alpha_y, t+1), v(a+\alpha_x, b+\alpha_y, t+1))$

assumed that the motion vectors of the four surrounding discrete positions are given by

$$\begin{aligned} \text{lower left} &= (u(a,b,t+1), v(a,b,t+1)) , \\ \text{lower right} &= (u(a+1,b,t+1), v(a+1,b,t+1)) , \\ \text{upper right} &= (u(a,b+1,t+1), v(a,b+1,t+1)) , \\ \text{lower left} &= (u(a+1,b+1,t+1), v(a+1,b+1,t+1)) . \end{aligned} \tag{4.9}$$

The interpolated motion vector $(u(a+\alpha_x, b+\alpha_y, t+1), v(a+\alpha_x, b+\alpha_y, t+1))$ corresponding to the position $(x+u(x,y,t), y+v(x,y,t), t+1)$ for is defined as

$$\begin{aligned} u(a+\alpha_x, b+\alpha_y, t+1) \;\; = \;\; & u(a,b,t+1)(1-\alpha_x)(1-\alpha_y) \\ & + u(a+1,b,t+1)\alpha_x(1-\alpha_y) \\ & + u(a,b+1,t+1)(1-\alpha_x)\alpha_y \\ & + u(a+1,b+1,t+1)\alpha_x\alpha_y , \end{aligned} \tag{4.10}$$

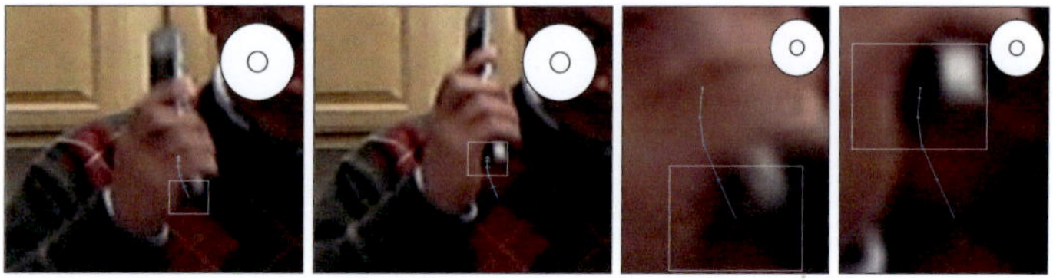

Figure 4.8.: Example for one trajectory based on bilinear interpolation for the action 'answer phone'

$$\begin{aligned} v(a+\alpha_x, b+\alpha_y, t+1) &= v(a,b,t+1)(1-\alpha_x)(1-\alpha_y) \\ &+ v(a+1,b,t+1)\alpha_x(1-\alpha_y) \\ &+ v(a,b+1,t+1)(1-\alpha_x)\alpha_y \\ &+ v(a+1,b+1,t+1)\alpha_x\alpha_y \,. \end{aligned} \tag{4.11}$$

With a computational complexity of $O(n)$, bilinear interpolation provides a good tradeoff between precision and speed. An example for the resulting trajectories is given inf Fig. 4.8. To show the improvement of subpixel interpolation over a discrete accumulation of the optical flow, the end points of several tracks has been evaluated and compared to hand annotated ground truth. Fig. 4.9 shows the comparison of the two methods. The subpixel interpolation shows a mean error of 8.9 pixels whereas the discrete accumulation of flow vectors results in a mean error of 13.3 pixels. The computation of the final motion vector is done by repeating this step for each following motion vector at the related position, until the desired length is reached. For this work, feature lengths of 2, 5, 10 and 20 frames were used, representing temporal a cropping of 133.3 ms up to 1.3 sec.

4.4. Feature quantization

Detection of areas with significant motion information leads to a varying number of features for each frame. An example of the feature distribution for a sample video with the activity "answer phone" is shown in Fig. 4.10. To be able to process this information in a recognition framework, the features have to be sampled to get to a fixed size frame representation. To

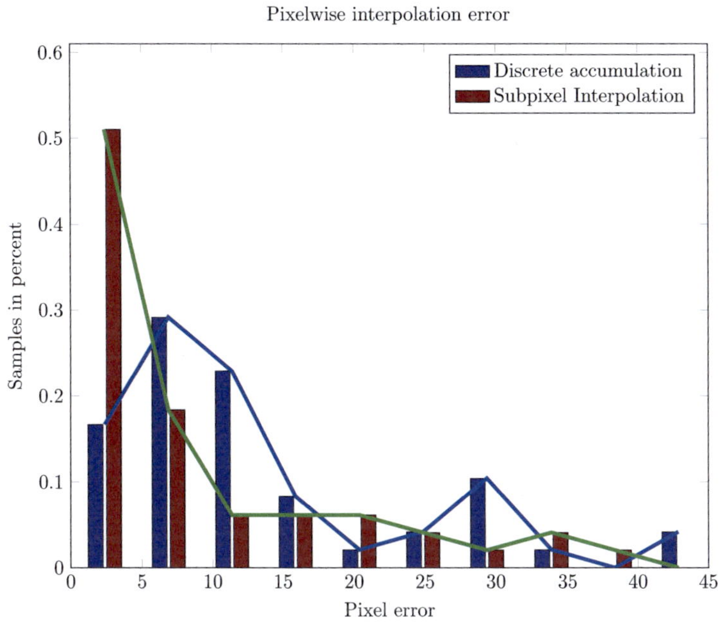

Figure 4.9.: Distribution of interpolation error of subpixel interpolation and discrete accumulation. More than half of the tracks based on subpixel interpolation show a pixel error of less than five pixels.

convert the resulting vectors into a fixed size frame representation, different methods have been developed and evaluated. The two main directions of building a frame signature from an inconsistent number of features is the accumulation of feature either by fixed sized bin histograms (see 4.4.1, p. 72) or by cluster centers gained from a subset of the training data (see 4.4.2, p. 75). In the first case, the histograms are built by a naïve sampling of motion directions. For the second, the bag-of words approach, the histogram is based on the accumulation of features in a clustered feature space. For this representation a number of random features is drawn from the training set and clustered into a number of clusters. To build the signature histogram of a frame, each feature is assigned to the closest cluster

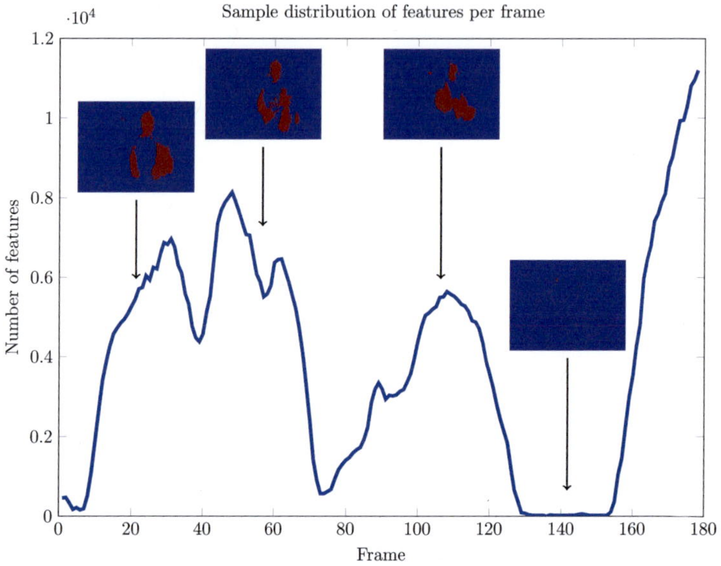

Figure 4.10.: Example for the feature distribution of a sample video with the activity "answer phone".

center. The histogram over all assignments represents the final signature of the frame.

In the following, different clustering and accumulation techniques are proposed, showing that a bag-of-words approach produces better overall recognition results for temporal crops than a naïve clustering by directions.

4.4.1. Clustering by Fixed Motion Direction

Simple Motion Direction

For a motion based clustering, the weighted histogram for frame t is calculated from the flow features $N_t = \{v_1, v_2, \ldots, v_n\}$ of image I at time index t.

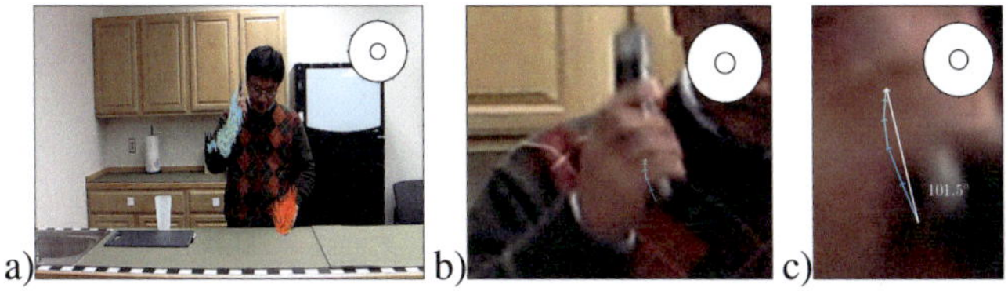

Figure 4.11.: Example for the computation of motion direction representation for the action "answer phone"

The motion direction θ of the related flow feature v_i is computed by considering the end position of the related feature vector

$$\theta(v_i) = \text{atan2}(\sum_{j=1}^{f} v_i(v_j), \sum_{j=1}^{f} v_i(u_j)). \quad (4.12)$$

The resulting angle value is in the range of $[0, 2\pi)$.

The elements for one bin of the histogram are calculated based on the motion angle θ. The vector of elements for the k-th bin $h(k)$ of a histogram with n bins is defined as

$$h_k = \left\{ v_i | \theta(v_i) \geq \frac{k2\pi}{n} - \pi \text{ and } \theta(v_i) < \frac{(k+1)2\pi}{n} - \pi \right\} . \quad (4.13)$$

Fig. 4.11 a) shows an example for the action "answer phone" as well as for the construction of one single trajectory. The trajectory over five frames is made up of 5 concatenated motion vectors (see Fig. 4.11 b)) and the overall trajectory is approximated by its end position (see Fig. 4.11 c)).

Motion Direction Including Length

To include the speed or intensity of a vector as additional knowledge, the motion intensity γ is computed as the distance from start to end position of

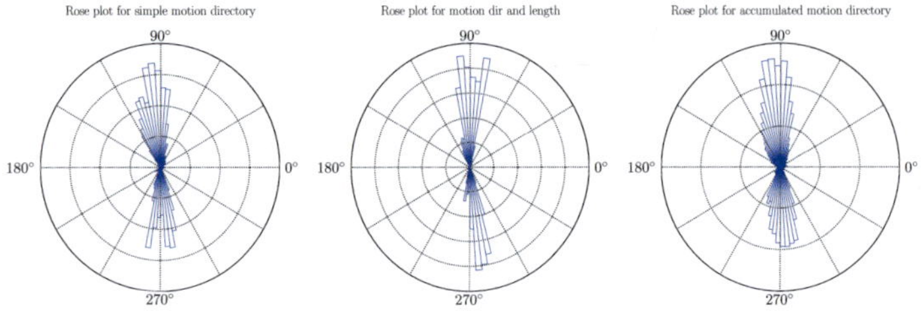

Figure 4.12.: Plot of the histogram of motion vectors based on simple motion direction, motion direction including length and accumulated motion direction.

the flow feature (see Fig. 4.11 c)) by

$$\gamma(v_i) = \sqrt{(\sum_{j=1}^{f} v_i(v_j))^2 + (\sum_{j=1}^{f} v_i(u_j))^2} = ||v_i||. \tag{4.14}$$

The elements for one bin of the histogram are calculated based on the motion angle θ. The bin entries are weighted with the related motion intensity. The k-th bin for the weighted histogram is calculated from the intensity of all elements in the vector as shown in

$$H(k) = \sum_{i=1}^{n_k} \gamma(h_k(i)) \,, \tag{4.15}$$

where n_k is the number of elements of the vector for the k-th bin h_k (see equ. 4.13).

Accumulated Motion Direction

In case of quantizing accumulative motion direction, the process is similar to quantization by simple motion direction, but here, no simplified trajectory is used. Instead, all motion vectors of the trajectory are quantized independently. This leads in case of a flow feature over five frames to five different histogram entries.

A comparison of the three different quantization techniques for the sample frame shown in Fig. 4.11 a) is given in Fig. 4.12. It shows that quantization by including the motion length pronounces the two main motion directions whereas an accumulated quantization of the feature vector also includes more angle information about the evolution of the motion within the regarded time span. Also, the overall speed and quantity of the two motion directions is better represented.

4.4.2. Bag-of-words Approach

The bag of words method can be seen as a standard feature quantization method and is widely used in different contexts. It was first proposed by Salton as "A Vector Space Model for Automatic Indexing" [SWY75] in context of document indexing to build a compact description of documents. The idea is to represent a document in form of a vector, whereas each dimension in the vector corresponds to a word and the entry at this dimension to the respective word count in the document. The resulting vector is a representation of the original document frequencies without information about its grammar or word order.

The idea has been adapted to the case of image based object classification by Csurka et al. [CBDF04]. Here, similar to Salton, any global or local contextual information is dropped in favor of "word" frequencies. The idea is to build visual object descriptions, or in this case general motion descriptions, out of a set of typical repetitive patches or features, corresponding to words in the vector space model. To find a representative set of patches, a number of them is first randomly drawn from the training data set. The randomly drawn features are clustered into k groups, whereas the center of each group is seen as a representative feature or word. To build the description of an object or a motion from those representative patches, all features of the related image or video volume are assigned to the closest cluster center. The quantization of this mapping is the final vector.

To apply the bag-of-words approach to flow-based features, a fixed number of random flow features is drawn from the training set. The features are clustered into k cluster using a k-means clustering. The distance between the feature vector v and the cluster center c can be expressed by

$$D(v,c) = \sqrt{\sum_{i=1}^{n}(v(i) - c(i))^2}\,, \tag{4.16}$$

where n corresponds to the number of elements in v resp. c. To build the flow feature histogram H for each frame t, all features of this frame are assigned to their closest cluster center C by

$$C(v) = \underset{c \in C}{\operatorname{argmin}}(D(v,c))\,. \tag{4.17}$$

The histogram is built by hard assignment of each feature to its cluster center:

$$h_k(v) = \begin{cases} 1, & C(v) = k \\ 0, & C(v) \neq k \end{cases}\,, \tag{4.18}$$

where

$$H(k) = \sum_{i=1}^{n_k} h_k(i) \tag{4.19}$$

and n_k corresponds to the number of elements in the k-th bin h_k. One can see that the number of bins is necessarily identical to the number of cluster centers.

For flow features, the results of the clustering process can be visualized, e.g. by sample trajectories of different clusters as displayed in Fig. 4.13. It shows that the clustering is mainly following the motion direction.

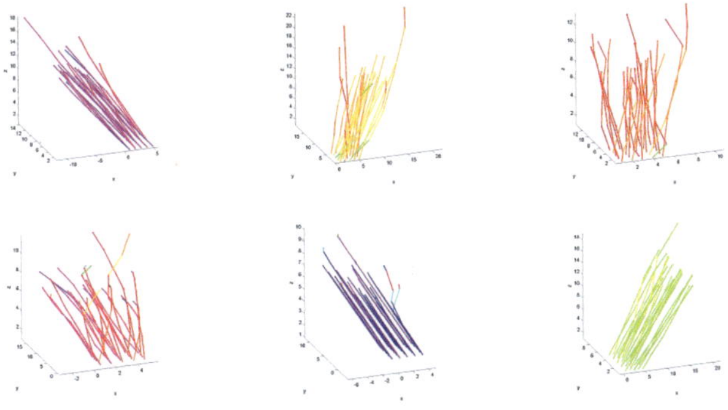

Figure 4.13.: Visualization of sample flow features of different clusters.

4.4.3. Evaluation of Feature Quantization Methods

To compare the different quantization strategies a classification framework has been set up. Therefore, the flow features of the ADL dataset have been sampled, first by fixed motion directions, using simple motion direction for the binning, as well as the combination of motion direction and length and the accumulated motion direction. The final histogram is built from the complete video, using all flow features of the video for one histogram. The same has been done for a bag of words approach, but in this case, first a number of 100000 features have been clustered in as many cluster centers as bins for the sampling by fixed motion direction and the cluster centers were used as "words" for the respective histogram. Classification is done by SVM [CL11] and random forest [Bre01]. The evaluation allows to assess the performance differences among the different sampling methods using the ADL dataset as reference dataset.

The results for the binning by fixed motion directions are shown in Tab. 4.2. It compares the recognition accuracy using simple motion direction (mdir), motion direction including length (mdir+length) and accumulated motion direction (acc. mdir) as described in sec. 4.4.1 for a classification by SVM and random forest (RF). One can see that binning by simple motion direction leads to the lowest accuracy compared to the binning of motion direction in combination with the overall feature length as well as binning of the accumulated feature vector. For all three cases best results are gained by a random forest classification with 30 bins. In a second step the two

ADL dataset					
Evaluation of motion direction with fixed sampling					
	cluster:	30c	50c	100c	200c
mdir 5 frames	SVM	17.33%	29.33%	29.33%	24.66%
	RF	**39.33**%	38.00 %	38.00%	**39.33**%
mdir+length 5 frames	SVM	24.66%	21.33%	23.33 %	12.66%
	RF	**42.00** %	40.00 %	40.67 %	40.00%
acc. mdir 5 frames	SVM	26.66%	26.00%	23.33 %	16.66%
	RF	**41.33** %	38.00 %	36.67 %	36.67%

Table 4.2.: Comparison of recognition accuracy for different binning methods based on motion direction.

better representations, motion direction including length (mdir+length) and accumulated motion direction (acc. mdir), were quantized in a bag-of-words manner as described in sec. 4.4.2. The results for SVM and random forest (RF) classification are shown in Tab. 4.3. One can see that a bag-of-words sampling clearly outperforms sampling by fixed motion directions for both methods (mdir+length +24.0%, acc. mdir +12.0%), showing overall better results for the representation of motion direction and length than for the accumulated motion direction.

The sampling by bag of words leads to a more uniform distribution of features and thus, to a more specific representation. Additionally, one can assume that the k-means clustering itself produces better results in this context, as flow features are, with 10 - 20 dimensions, rather low dimensional descriptors. Thus, clustering in 10 dimensional space will result in more coherent clusters than the clustering of high-level descriptors with 100 dimensions and more. Therefore, it can be expected that the influence

ADL dataset					
Evaluation of motion direction with BOW sampling					
		30c	50c	100c	200c
mdir + length 5 frames	SVM:	48.00%	49.33%	52.67%	52.67%
	RF:	52.00%	62.00%	59.33%	**66.00%**
acc. mdir 5 frames	SVM:	50.00%	**53.33%**	50.00%	52.67%
	RF:	40.00%	44.67%	46.00%	46.00%
acc. mdir 10 frames	SVM:	52.67%	55.33%	54.67%	**56.00%**
	RF:	44.00%	47.33%	44.00%	46.00%

Table 4.3.: Comparison of recognition accuracy for different binning methods based on motion direction.

of the clustering procedure is more significant in this context than for other features.

Finally, the third evaluation (Tab. 4.4) shows the recognition results for the case that the vectors of original flow features as described in sec. 4.3 were used for the clustering and matched to their related cluster center. One can see that this form of flow feature clustering again increases the recognition performance by +10% compared to the clustering of the combination of motion direction and length. To further evaluate this approach, the method has been tested for the case of 3, 5 and 10 frames, showing the best results for 5 and 10 frames. Based on those results this configuration is used for the further evaluation of the features as well as for the final proposed system.

ADL dataset					
Evaluation of flow features with BOW sampling					
	cluster:	30c	50c	100c	200c
flow features 3 frames	SVM:	56.67%	51.33%	53.33%	47.33%
	RF:	68.00%	62.67%	**68.67**%	67.33%
flow features 5 frames	SVM:	53.33%	62.67%	61.33%	63.33%
	RF:	64.67%	72.67%	**76.00**%	74.00%
flow features 10 frames	SVM:	40.67%	66.00%	64.67%	61.33%
	RF:	66.00%	69.33%	**76.00**%	74.67%

Table 4.4.: Comparison of recognition accuracy for different flow feature lengths and BOW sampling.

4.5. Evaluation of Flow Features

The proposed method has been evaluated on three different datasets namely the BKT dataset, the ADL dataset and the breakfast dataset, all varying in size, complexity and structure. As the BTK dataset, as the simplest of all, just shows staged actors with repetitive movements, the breakfast dataset comprises data records of 52 people working in real kitchens without any further constrains. Considering the size of the different dataset, there are about 100 clips in the Weizmann dataset and almost 2000 clips available for the breakfast dataset.

4.5.1. Evaluation of General Codebook Properties

To compare flow features to the state of the art descriptor, the following evaluation uses the HOGHOF feature descriptor gained by the Harris 3D corner detector as proposed by Laptev et al. [Lap05].

One has to remark that both features show different properties. Whereas the flow features can be seen as a representation of ongoing motion within a time frame, HOGHOF descriptors are patched based, thus represent local gradient and flow structures within the video. Also the detection of both feature types leads to different feature quantities considering the overall number of features per video and per frame which shows in different densities of the resulting histogram representation.

The overall number of detected features for all three datasets is show in Fig. 4.14. Considering all datasets, there is a mean of ~8 features per frame detected by the Harris corner detector, compared to a mean detection rate of ~329 flow features per frame. Overall, the mean detection rate for flow features is 40 times higher than the mean detection rate of the Harris corner detector. Looking at the rates of the different datasets, there are ~100 times more features available per frame considering the ADL dataset (11 HOGHOF, 1100 flow), ~140 time more for the BKT dataset (9 HOGHOF, 1300 Flow) and ~35 times more for the Breakfast dataset (7

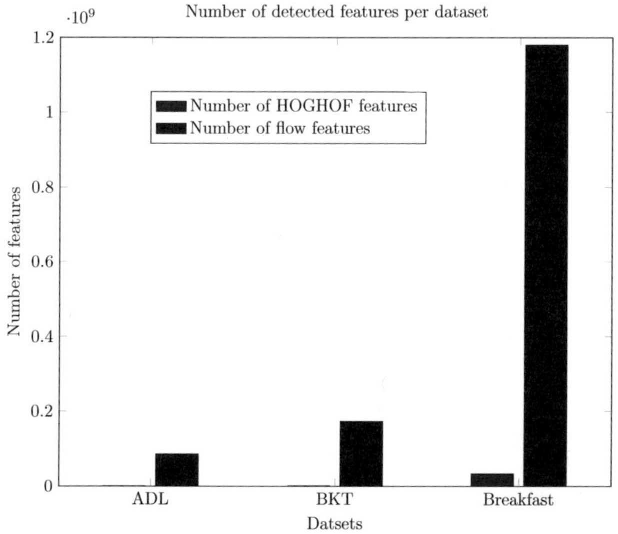

Figure 4.14.: Overall number of detected features for the three different datasets

HOGHOF, 300 Flow). The difference of flow features per frame for ADL and BKT dataset compared to the Breakfast dataset mainly results from the different resolution of both datasets. Hence the Breakfast dataset has only half the resolution of the other two, the number necessarily varies. After normalizing the scaling factor, it shows that also for this dataset, the number of features is very consistent, comparing the different setting of the datasets.

On the frame based level a low amount of HOGHOF features also leads necessary to an increased sparsity of the resulting histogram. To evaluate this effect and measure the overall histogram-per-frame sparsity, a number of random sample histograms have been drawn and the amount of bins with one or more entries has been determined. The results are shown in Fig. 4.15. One can see that with growing amount of bins, the number of entries that are not zeros decreases for HOGHOF features, whereas the amount of non-zero entries for flow features stays stable, even for larger binning

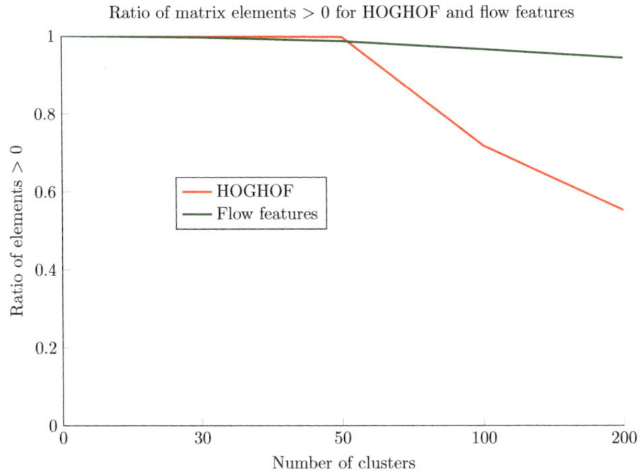

Figure 4.15.: Ratio of bins with one or more entries for HOGHOF and flow features

sizes. Further flow features have a lower dimensionality of 20 to 40 dimensions than HOGHOF features with 162 dimensions. This can lead to more consistent results in terms of clustering based on the curse of dimensionality as stated by Bellman [Bel61]. The effect of clustering flow features is visualized Fig. 4.16. The figure shows the first two components of the flow feature descriptor and the HOGHOF descriptor after clustering with color coded cluster mapping. Thus this comparison has only limited validity, one can see the difference in terms of cluster compactness for the flow features, whereas there are no visible clusters for HOGHOF features with 162 dimensions.

4.5.2. Reference System Description

To evaluate the classification performance of the proposed feature, a reference systems has been built based on the architecture described by Laptev et al. [LMSR08] and Wang et al. [WUK$^+$09]. It features a bag-of-words action recognition approach.

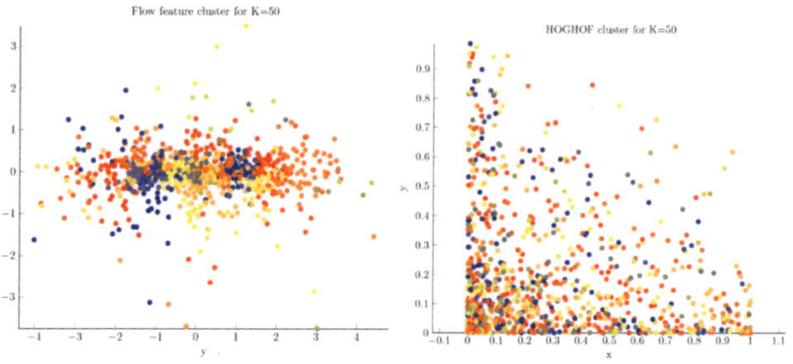

Figure 4.16.: Visualization of first two components of the flow feature descriptor and the HOGHOF descriptor after clustering with 30 cluster center.

First, 100000 features are randomly sampled for the training set and clustered into k clusters using a K-means implementation of Sorber et al. [Sor10] based on [Mac67] and [AV07].

The resulting cluster centers C are used as reference to build the frame or video signature of the train and test data. Therefore all features of the desired temporal window are assigned to their closest cluster centers based on Euclidean distance. The histogram is built over a time frame $[t-\frac{n}{2}, t+\frac{n}{2}]$ by hard assignment of each feature to its cluster center leading to a set of frame descriptors $\mathbf{x}$ with

$$\mathbf{x} = x_1, x_2, \ldots, x_T \tag{4.20}$$

per video, whereas each elements represents one histogram for each time frame.

For the case of the classification of complete sequences, the interval of $[t, t+n]$ is considered by setting t to 1 and n corresponding to the number of frames and the number of elements of $\mathbf{x}$ is one.

For the discriminative classification, two state-of-the-art classification methods, support vector machines and random forest, are used. The classification by support vector machines (SVM) is used widely in action recognition publications especially for benchmark implementations. The here proposed work uses the implementation of Chang and Lin [CL11] libSVM with a radial basis function $e^{(-\gamma * |u-v|^2)}$ as kernel function. Following the best practice guidelines as described in [HCL03], all data is first normalized and scaled to the closed interval of $[0,1]$. To estimate the best parameters for C and γ, a five fold cross validation is applied to the training data with the parameters $C = 2^{-5}, 2^{-3}, \ldots, 2^{13}, 2^{15}$ and $\gamma = 2^{-10}, 2^{-8}, \ldots, 2^{8}, 2^{10}$. To classify data with multiple class labels, the libsvm build in multiclass approach is used featuring a one-vs-one classification strategy in combination with a voting to combine the results of binary classification. One has to remark that in case of two classes having identical votes, the class appearing first in the array of storing class names is used (see [CL11], chp. 7). This explains a bias towards classes appearing at the beginning of a set, especially in combination with overall low recognition accuracy.

Additionally, the classification by random forests is used. Random forest are gaining more and more attention, especially since their successful application in context of the Microsoft Kinect™pose estimation approach [SFC⁺11]. The here reported results are based on the implementation of Breiman and Cutler [Bre01, BC13]. To evaluate the optimal number and depth of the decision trees, following the guidelines of [BC13], a 4-fold cross validation is applied to the training data for 200 and 300 trees and a depth of 16, 32 and 42 nodes per tree. The parameters with the highest recognition accuracy are chosen for training and recognition.

In case of imbalanced training data, as it arises for unit- and frame-based classification, different over- and undersampling techniques based on [HG09] have been implemented and compared to the weighting functions provided by the discriminative classifiers [HCL03, BC13]. Here, the Synthetic Minority Over-sampling Technique (SMOTE) [CBHK02] shows the best performance and is therefore chosen for the following evaluation. Additionally, to avoid an oversampling by too many artificially generated data, the training data of classes with large amount of samples is limited to a maximum number of samples per class.

The here proposed reference implementation has been evaluated on a variety of different action recognition datasets (see [KJG$^+$11, KGSS12]) and produces state-of-the-art results on standard action recognition dataset.

4.5.3. Evaluation of ADL Dataset

In the following, all three datasets, as discussed in Chp.3, are considered for the evaluation of the proposed feature type. The start is made by the ADL dataset. Recognition accuracy on unit as well as on sequence level is used to assess its performance and characteristics, with focus on the recognition performance for the unit level.

This evaluation procedure is different from standard action recognition literature which usually only focuses on the recognition of the overall sequence. As overall sequence recognition only considers one label for the complete video sequence, such a recognition does to capture the underlying semantic structure of the video. One of the main advantages of the here presented approach is in the parsing and analysis of this structure. Thus, a simple evaluation of sequences accuracy would only capture one part of the overall system results. It can further be assumed that the recognition on unit level is a harder problem compared to overall sequence classification. Therefore, the following evaluation focuses on the unit recognition. For completeness and to allow comparability with other benchmarks, both results, the recognition accuracy on unit as well as on sequence level are reported.

Unit Recognition

To evaluate the quality of unit recognition for the proposed features each frame is represented by the histogram of flow and HOGHOF features over a sliding window of 10 frames. Unit recognition is done on frame level, assigning each frame of a clip to one of the 48 different action unit classes listed in the ADL dataset description (Sec. 3.4, p.3.4).

Because of different lengths and distribution of action units, a simple frame based sampling of test and training samples usually leads to a between-class imbalance. To avoid an imbalanced classification, the overall sampling is done by first choosing 1000 random samples from those classes with more than 1000 training samples and then complementing the samples of classes with less than 1000 samples by artificially generated samples using SMOTE.

The results are shown in Tab. 4.5. One can see that flow features perform better than HOGHOF descriptors, reaching a recognition rate of 29.41% at best, whereas HOGHOF performs only at 20.89%. As the evaluation has been done for low cluster dimensions and as HOGHOF have shown best result for rather higher cluster dimensions [WUK+09], HOGHOF features have also been evaluated for the case of a 2000 dimensional histogram, but with 20.49%, the overall recognition accuracy did not increase.

ADL dataset					
Frame-based unit accuracy					
HOGHOF					
cluster:	c30	c50	c100	c200	c400
SVM	16.58%	16.92%	19.77%	21.12%	20.05%
RF	17.43%	18.77%	21.16%	**21.75%**	20.49%
Flow (5f)					
cluster:	c30	c50	c100	c200	c400
SVM	20.04%	21.03%	21.50%	22.84%	20.80%
RF	23.20%	25.81%	25.67%	26.09%	**27.11%**
Flow (10f)					
cluster:	c30	c50	c100	c200	c400
SVM	21.31%	21.88%	23.15%	24.51%	23.94%
RF	23.38%	26.28%	26.51%	28.78%	**29.41%**

Table 4.5.: Comparison of Bag-of-words approach with HOGHOF and flow features. The accuracy shows, how many frames were associated to the right action unit (chance at 2.1%).

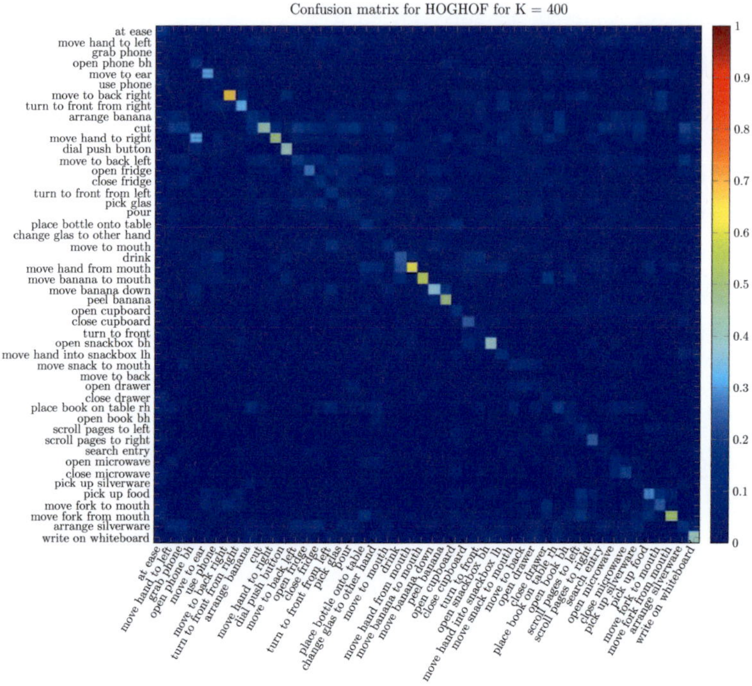

Figure 4.17.: Confusion matrix of the recognition accuracy of unit per frame based on HOGHOF

Looking at the results for the different action units as shown in Fig. 4.17 and 4.18, one can see that there are few units performing well at ~60% and more, whereas most of the units are not correctly recognized at all. Overall, it can also be seen that, in case of this more complex scenario, flow features outperform standard HOGHOF features when it comes to the recognition of temporally smaller entities and more classes. This might be due to the overall count of flow features compared to HOGHOF. But it can also be a hint that the higher dimensional, complex descriptor fails to capture the variety of differences, when it comes to a larger amount of classes, as there are approximately five times more unit classes (overall 48) than sequence classes (overall 10).

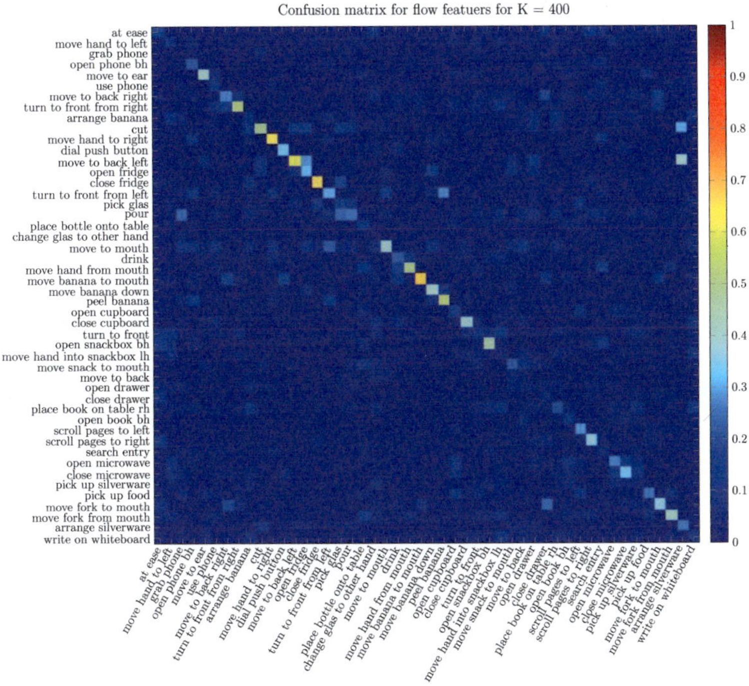

Figure 4.18.: Confusion matrix of the recognition accuracy of unit per frame based on flow features over 10 frames

Sequence Recognition

For the classification of complete action sequences, histograms were sampled over all features of a complete video and classes were defined based on the original label of the video, e.g. “answer phone” or “drink water”, resulting in 10 different classes for the ADL dataset. Overall, one can see that the HOGHOF descriptor performs best with 86.67% for a codebook size of $2000K$ whereas the best performance of flow features with 76.00% is reached with a codebook size of $100K$. Overall, in case of complete sequence recognition with discriminative classifiers, HOGHOF outperforms simple flow features. One can make several assumptions, what

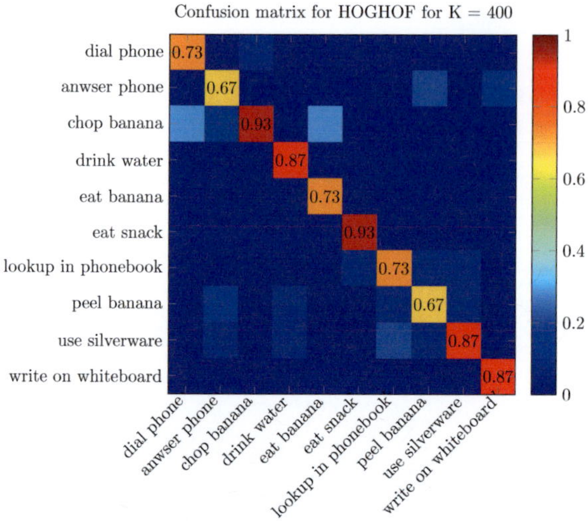

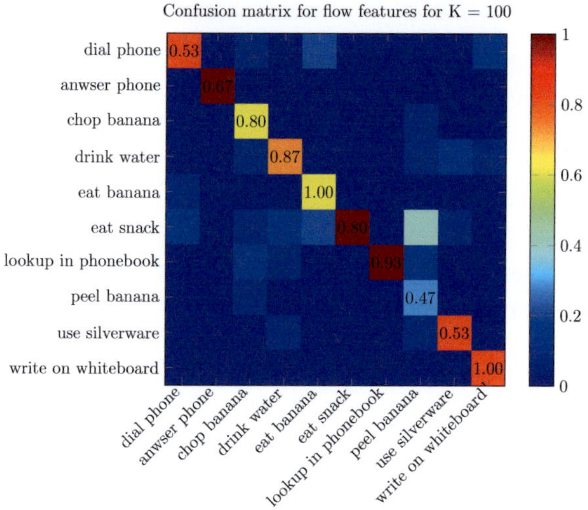

Figure 4.19.: Confusion matrix of the recognition accuracy of full sequences based on HOGHOF and flow features over 10 frames

ADL dataset						
Sequence recognition accuracy						
HOGHOF						
cluster:	c30	c50	c100	c200	c400	c2000
SVM	72.67 %	80.00 %	80.67%	84.00%	80.00%	84.00%
RF	66.67%	71.33%	76.67%	81.33%	86.00%	**86.67%**
Flow (5f)						
cluster:	c30	c50	c100	c200	c400	c2000
SVM	53.33%	62.76%	61.33%	63.33%	64.67%	66.67%
RF	64.67%	72.67%	**76.00%**	74.00%	72.67%	73.33%
Flow (10f)						
cluster:	c30	c50	c100	c200	c400	c2000
SVM	40.67%	66.00%	64.67%	61.33%	68.00%	68.67%
RF	66.00%	69.33%	**76.00%**	74.67%	73.33%	76.00%

Table 4.6.: Comparison of Bag-of-words approach with HOGHOFs and flow features using SVM and Random Forest classification

the better performance of the HOGHOF descriptor compared to flow features in this case could be based on. First, for the case of classifying full video sequences, all features of the complete video sequence are sampled in one histogram. The resulting HOGHOF descriptor is not as sparse as it is for a frame-wise sampling. This advantage of the HOGHOF features in terms of full sequences can also be seen as a disadvantage of the flow features. Here, the sampling of all features from the video can lead to an oversampling, and mixing up all occurring motions in one histogram might not lead to an appropriate representation of the activity itself. Second, when considering the complete sequences, elements different from the pure motion information might be taken into account in case of the HOGHOF descriptor. As HOGHOF also encodes shape, it is appropriate to assume that the final histogram does not only include motion information, but also shape information about the objects used in this activity. The shape information might not play a role when it comes to unit recognition, because here, a lot of different units share the same object, e.g. "peel banana", "put banana to mouth", and "grab banana". But when it comes to the recognition of complete activities, object information can be a valuable cue and is implicitly represented in the HOGHOF based histogram.

Comparison to Public Benchmarks

Further, as the ADL dataset has been widely used a public benchmark, the results may also be compared to other approaches presented in Tab. 4.7. There are two points to remark. Current approaches score around ~80% recognition accuracy (see Tab. 4.7). Only Augmented Velocity Histories [MPK09], which include additional absolute position information reach a recognition rate of 89% for the price of depending on correct location of the test persons. The recognition rate in this case might considerably drop as soon as the tasks were executed at locations different from the predefined ones.

ADL dataset	
	Accuracy
HOGHOF [LMSR08] (impl. by [MPK09])	59%
Velocity Histories (VH) [MPK09]	63%
Latent VH [MPK09]	67%
Augmented VH (incl. abs. pos.) [MPK09]	89%
Temporal cropping (HOF) [MHS10]	80.0%
Tracklets [RS10]	82.7%
HOGHOF [LMSR08] (reference implementation)	86.67%
Flow features	76.00%

Table 4.7.: Recognition performance of different approaches for the ADL dataset as reported by the authors. First section shows recognition accuracy of different methods as reported in the authors of the dataset. Second section shows results of other groups and the last section shows best accuracy of the reference implementation used in this work for HOGHOF and flow features

Second, one has to remark that the recognition accuracy for HOGHOF features reached by the presented implementation is considerably higher than in the original paper. The results of the here presented implementation are consistent with the comparison of Velocity Histories(VH) and HOGHOF features conducted by the authors themselves[MPK09] on the KTH dataset, where HOGHOF features performed with 80% recognition accuracy ∼6% better then Velocity Histories with 74% and can therefore assumed to be correct despite deviating results published by [MPK09]. Additionally, it shows that the reference implementation based on HOGHOF features that the new proposed flow features are compared with can be seen as state-of-the-art method.

4.5.4. Evaluation of BKT Dataset

The same evaluation as described in Sec. 4.5.3 has also been conducted for the BKT dataset. The BKT dataset can be considered as an easier one, as it only involves one test person performing simple structured tasks. Nevertheless, one can see that, even in such a limited setting, a frame based parsing can be a challenging problem.

Unit Recognition

For the frame based classification first, the histogram distribution is computed for each frame, based on the features of a sliding window of ten frames. The class of a frame is given by the respective unit level, e.g. "take knife", "pouring", "put bowl away", resulting in an overall of 43 different action units for the BKT dataset.

To balance the training data, a combination of cutoff and minority oversampling as described in the previous section is used.

The overall recognition accuracy by frame per unit reaches at best 54% for a codebook of 200K for HOGHOF and 59.47% for flow features. Overall one can see a remarkably drop compared to the recognition results of the complete action sequences.

Looking at the recognition results for the single classes in detail, as shown in Fig. 4.20 and 4.21, one can see that the overall recognition is

BKT dataset				
Frame-based unit accuracy				
HOGHOF				
cluster:	c30	c50	c100	c200
SVM	38.82%	43.93%	48.66%	53.55%
RF	41.48%	44.71%	49.97%	**54.00%**
Flow (5f)				
cluster:	c30	c50	c100	c200
SVM	46.89%	51.66%	56.42%	58.53%
RF	55.11%	58.56%	**59.47%**	59.11%

Table 4.8.: Results for frame-based classification of 46 different action units on the BKT dataset comparing HOGHOF and flow features without temporal modeling. Results are reported for SVM and Random Forest classification

better than for the ADL dataset. For both cases mainly neighboring units tend to be mixed up, which can be induced by temporal overlaps around the segment borders. Additionally, HOGHOF features rather confuse the different pick and place operations, probably because of their visual similarity, especially when the involved object is very small like a fruit or a piece of cake.

Sequence Recognition

For sequences recognition, classes were defined based on the label of the overall video, e.g. "cutting fruits" or "pouring water", resulting in 10 different classes for the BKT dataset. The result of the overall classification is shown in Tab. 4.6. One can see that HOGHOF features show a $\sim$4% better recognition accuracy than flow features with the classical bag-of-words approach scoring a perfect 100% with a codebook size of $100K$ or higher.

The respective confusion matrix for flow features thus shows that there is no specific trend regarding the misclassifications of the single activities. Instead several activities get mix up with each other like "cutting" and "rolling" or "slicing" and "sawing". This can be seen as another hint

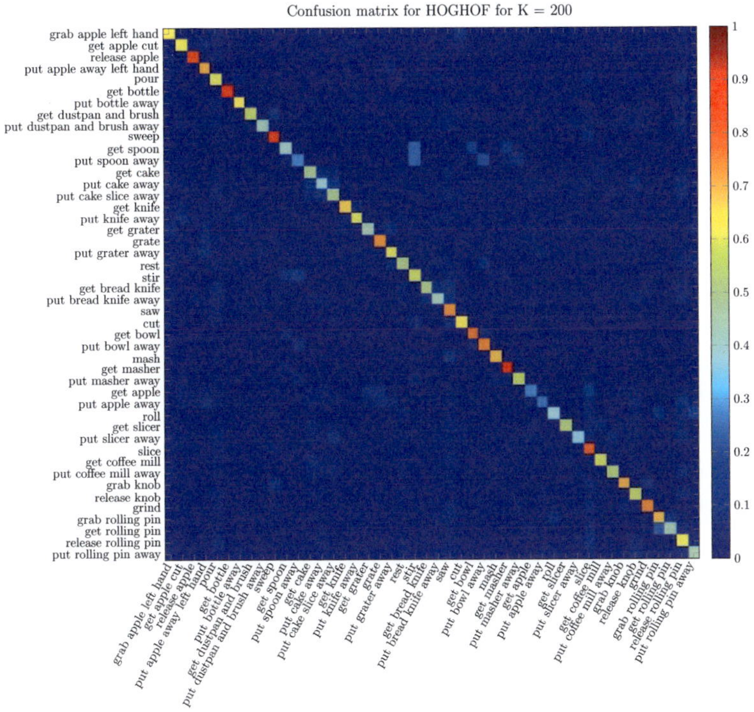

Figure 4.20.: Confusion matrix of the recognition accuracy of unit per frame based on HOGHOF

that, in case of sequence recognition, the accumulated flow features tend to become too unspecific and are thus difficult to separate by a discriminative classifier.

4.5.5. Evaluation of Breakfast Dataset

Compared to the two preceding datasets, the Breakfast dataset is richer and more complex, comprising 52 test persons recorded at 18 different locations with different view points. Poor results in unit recognition accuracy show, that a frame based classification without any structural knowledge is not feasible for this kind of real-world data.

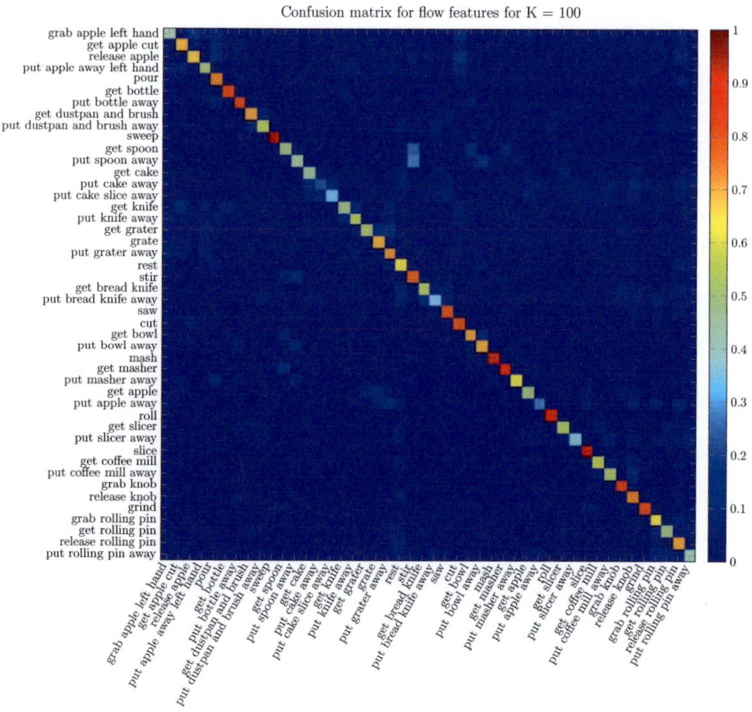

Figure 4.21.: Confusion matrix of the recognition accuracy of unit per frame based on flow features

Unit Recognition

The complexity and heterogeneity of the dataset becomes clear when looking the unit accuracy, which is at 6.33% for flow features and 6.40% for HOGHOF features. As ~6% recognition accuracy are only slightly above chance level (~2%) the evaluation clearly shows that discriminative methods for both feature types fail at this task. This becomes even clearer when looking at the confusion matrix for the best scoring configuration in shown in Fig. 4.23 and 4.23. One can see that nothing, except one respectively two classes, is recognized at a significant level. This drop can be attributed to the increased complexity of the dataset. Compared to the two previous

BKT dataset				
Sequence recognition accuracy				
HOGHOF				
cluster:	c30	c50	c100	c200
SVM	98.26 %	99.13 %	**100.00 %**	**100.00 %**
RF	99.57 %	98.26 %	**100.00 %**	**100.00 %**
Flow (5f)				
cluster:	c30	c50	c100	c200
SVM	94.00 %	93.60 %	95.20 %	96.80 %
RF	94.00 %	93.60 %	95.20 %	**96.80** %

Table 4.9.: Results for the BKT datasets with 10 action classes comparing HOGHOF and flow features without temporal modeling. Results are reported for SVM and Random Forest classification

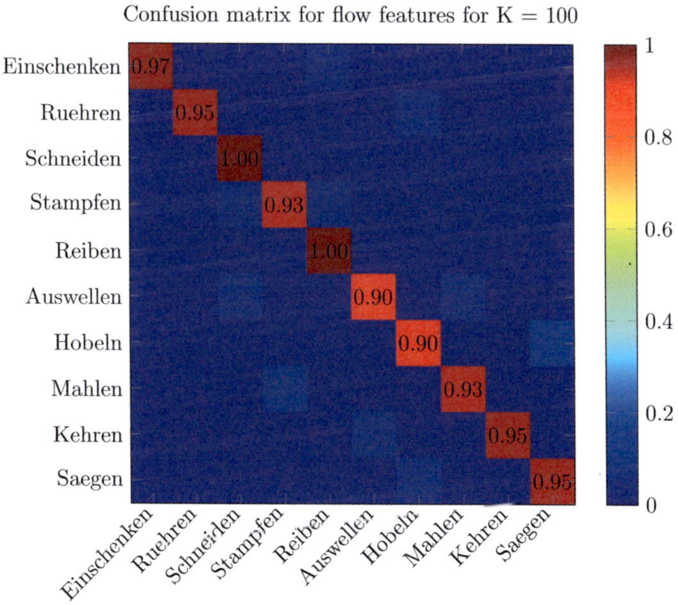

Figure 4.22.: Confusion matrix of the recognition accuracy of activities based on flow features

Breakfast dataset				
Frame-based unit accuracy				
HOGHOF				
cluster:	c30	c50	c100	c200
SVM	3.99%	4.84%	5.44%	3.89%
RF	5.56%	5.68%	6.09%	**6.40%**
Flow (5f)				
cluster:	c30	c50	c100	c200
SVM	3.68%	4.81%	5.38%	4.17%
RF	5.00%	5.52%	**6.33%**	5.65%

Table 4.10.: Comparison of Bag-of-words approach with HOGOHF and flow features and SVM and Random Forest unit classification for unit recognition. Only results for mirrored clips are reported.

datasets, the Breakfast dataset has been recorded at 18 different locations, thus even relative location information, for example about the position of furniture or tools, can not be used as a cue for classification. Additionally, the complexity of the sequences has increased compared to the previous datasets. Considering the number of units per sequence in general, but also the number of possible combinations, as the recordings were less restricted and people acted more naturally than in a lab scenario. Finally, the overall number of test persons has been increased from one resp. five persons to 52 different test persons, making this dataset also more variable as each person has not only a different body structure but also different motion patterns and behavior up to different skills and levels of practice when it comes to the preparation of food.

Sequence Recognition

The proposed features have additionally been used to evaluate the sequence recognition of the Breakfast dataset. The overall recognition accuracy for the 10 different action sequences is shown in Tab. 4.11. It can be seen that the recognition accuracy for HOGHOF (29.23%) and flow features (26.00%) are considerably lower than for the first two datasets.

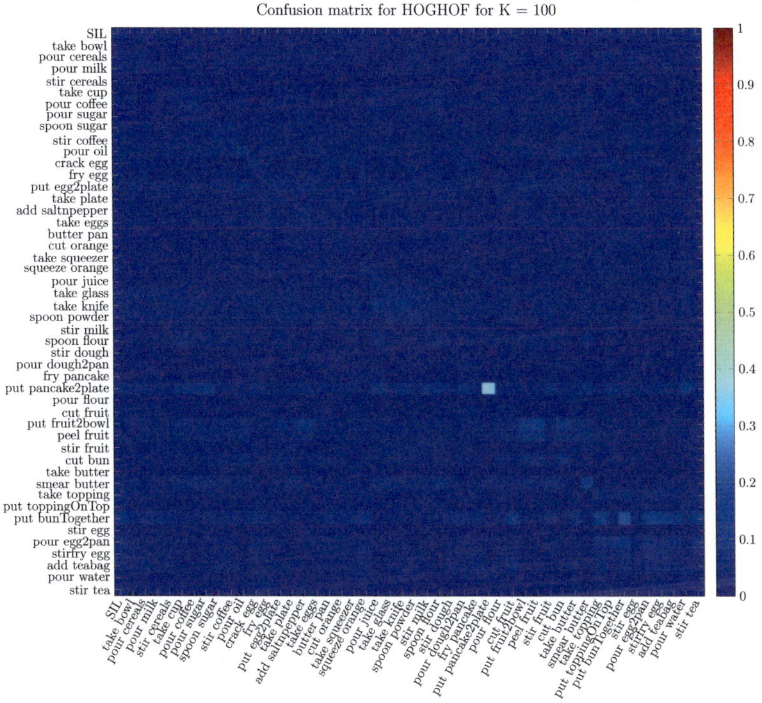

Figure 4.23.: Confusion matrix of the recognition accuracy of unit per frame based on HOGHOF and flow features over 10 frames

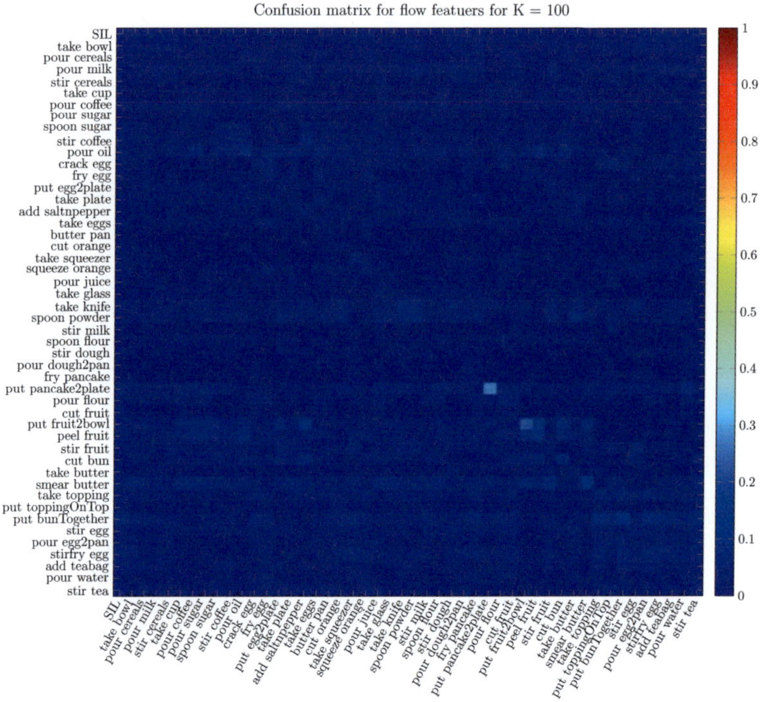

Figure 4.24.: Confusion matrix of the recognition accuracy of unit per frame based on HOGHOF and flow features over 10 frames

Breakfast dataset				
Sequence recognition accuracy				
HOGHOF				
cluster:	c30	c50	c100	c200
SVM	23.30%	21.65%	25.23%	**29.23**%
RF	19.76%	21.65%	24.75%	27.18%
HOGHOF mirrored				
cluster:	c30	c50	c100	c200
SVM	25.15%	**26.04**%	21.53%	21.03%
RF	22.72%	23.96%	20.93%	22.72%
Flow (5f)				
cluster:	c30	c50	c100	c200
SVM	20.95%	21.00%	18.67%	19.31 %
RF	22.17%	20.87%	24.05%	**25.37**%
Flow (5f) mirrored				
cluster:	c30	c50	c100	c200
SVM	22.34%	21.74%	23.20%	**26.00**%
RF	18.08%	21.62%	22.41%	25.09%

Table 4.11.: Comparison of Bag-of-words approach with HOGHOF and flow features and SVM and Random Forest classification of complete sequences for mirrored and non mirrored clips

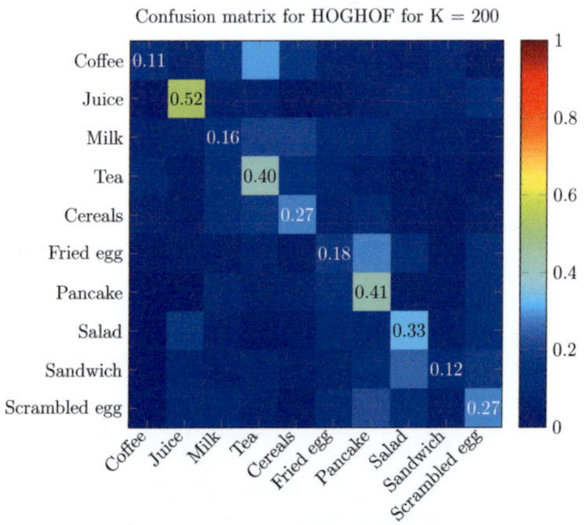

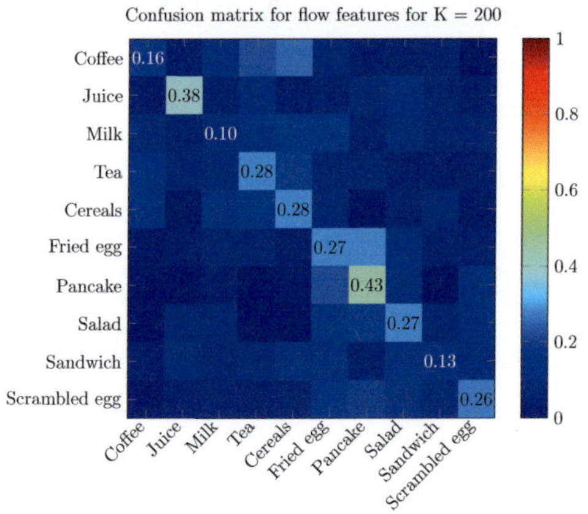

Figure 4.25.: Confusion matrix of the recognition accuracy for Breakfast sequence for units per frame based on HOGHOF and flow features over 10 frames

4.6. Conclusion

The chapter presented a descriptor for human actions based on flow information that provides good results for the recognition of short action units.

First motion information based on optical flow is computed and concatenated over time resulting in a number of flow vectors for each frame. As this representation also includes a lot of static background, the problem arises that not all extracted flow vectors are relevant for the recognition of the ongoing motion. Therefore, different detection techniques have been applied and evaluated to sample frames of the three sequences. Overall it showed that a detection based on the extracted flow features in combination with a cumulative threshold performs best, leading to an overall precision of 79.51% with a recall of 57.09%.

After flow features in regions with no significant motion a removed and only features in regions with significant motion are kept, the number of features per frame necessarily varies from frame to frame. As the following recognition stages require a low dimensional frame representation with a fixed number of dimensions, the resulting features need to be aggregated in one single vector. For this quantization process different binning criteria from angle based to bag of words approaches are considered and evaluated, showing that a bag-of-words approach on the overall features provides the best recognition accuracy for this type of feature.

The second part of this chapter deals with the evaluation of the proposed features on the three reference dataset. Therefore, the recognition accuracy of the proposed feature as well as of the HOGHOF descriptor is evaluated in context of a discriminative recognition framework. For classification, two state-of-the-art classifiers are used, support vector machines and random forests. It shows that on the unit recognition level the proposed feature is able to outperform the state-of-the-art HOGHOF descriptor on the ADL and the BKT dataset. On the breakfast dataset, both descriptors perform equally in terms of unit recognition. In terms of sequence classification, the best recognition performances varies with a trend towards HOGHOF features.

Overall it shows that the proposed descriptor is especially suitable for the recognition of smaller entities and thus, a good choice for a recognition approach based on unit recognition as described in the following chapter.

5. Temporal modeling

So far, the evaluation of features was based only on single frames or video clips without considering any temporal information.

The following chapter goes beyond this simplified structure and describes the modeling, training, and recognition of video sequences over time. Therefore, techniques from automatic speech recognition, namely HMMs and grammars, are adapted to the case of video based action recognition. An example for the application of those technique in context of speech recognition has e.g. been given by Rabiner [Rab89, RJ86]. The paper discusses the three fundamental problems for HMM design: the evaluation of the probability of a sequence of observations given a specific HMM, which is known as the evaluation problem; the determination of a best sequence of modeling states, which is known as decoding problem; and the adjustment of model parameters in order to maximize the probability of a sequence of observations, which is known as learning problem. In context of the here proposed video analysis, the evaluation problem corresponds to the problem of computing the probability of a specific unit given a set of input vectors. The decoding problem corresponds to the problem of finding the best possible sequence of states, and on a higher level of units, given a related the input vector. And the learning problem corresponds to the problem of training an HMM, given a set of samples.

For the implementation of the presented concepts, the open source speech recognition framework HTK[1] proposed by Young et al. [YEG+06] is used. The elements of the system described in the following are based on the concepts of phoneme recognition and parsing and adapted for the usage of

[1]Hidden Markov Toolkit (HTK) 3.4.1, University of Cambridge, 2012

frame based representations of human actions instead of speech signals. As the focus of this work lies in the transfer of action recognition onto existing methods and not in the design of new recognition systems, HMM-based modeling and continuous sequence recognition are only discussed as far as it is necessary to understand the transfer process.

The chapter is built as follows: First, a general discussion of the processing of video signals over time is given in Sec. 5.1. The modeling of action units is described in Sec. 5.2 as well as the global modeling of action sequences in Sec. 5.3. The evaluation of the proposed approach is described in Sec. 5.4, followed by the conclusion in Sec. 5.5.

5.1. Recognition and Processing of Actions Over Time

In most action classification approaches, the representation of a video, e.g. in form of features points or frame representations, is treated as a set of observations without any local or temporal relation. Classification is usually done over all data points regardless the internal structure like the appearance of features over time. But as a video input can be seen as a type of sequential data, namely the visual representation of a scene at successive time frames, a temporal modeling of the data can provide a better representation of the input data than a global model. Additionally, a temporal model can lead to some insights, a global model would not necessary provide like the representation of the input data over time.

As motion is defined as a displacement during a time interval, so far only captures the resulting displacement is considered. To model the temporal extend of the ongoing motion, the here presented approach refers to concepts used in speech processing, namely the concatenation of smaller units, which can be compared to phones in speech recognition into larger sequences, which can be compared to words or sentences. Therefore video sequences are first split into smaller action units, which can be combined into larger sequences following a predefined grammar.

Applying those concepts onto action representations gained from video sequences allows further to make a direct use of tools and techniques of automatic speech recognition. Parallel to phonemes in speech processing, action units are modeled as HMMs. The units are than combined by connecting their representation. As the occurrence of those units, comparable to speech, usually follows specific rules, those rules are defined by an action grammar.

5.2. Modeling of Action Units

In order to model action units over time, we assume that the feature vector holds a sequence of frame representations that represent the ongoing motion at that time. The task of recognizing an action unit is therefore defined by finding the best match of the input sequence $\mathbf{x}$ with

$$\mathbf{x} = x_1, x_2, \ldots, x_T \tag{5.1}$$

with x_i representing the feature vector at frame t, to a given number of action units u

$$\mathbf{u} = u_1, u_2, \ldots, u_N \ . \tag{5.2}$$

This can be formulated as maximizing the probability of an action unit u_i , given the input sequence $\mathbf{x}$

$$\underset{i \in 1,\ldots,N}{\operatorname{argmax}} P(u_i|\mathbf{x}) \tag{5.3}$$

with the a posteriori probability

$$P(u_i|\mathbf{x}) = \frac{P(\mathbf{x}|u_i)P(u_i)}{P(\mathbf{x})} \ . \tag{5.4}$$

with $P(\mathbf{x}|u_i)$, $P(u_i)$ and $P(\mathbf{x})$ is the observation probability of the given sequence $\mathbf{x}$. As the observation probability of the current sequence $\mathbf{x}$ is the same for all units, it is usually omitted and only the a posteriori likelihood

$$P(u_i|\mathbf{x}) = P(\mathbf{x}|u_i)P(u_i) \; . \tag{5.5}$$

is considered.

The unit probability $P(u_i)$ can be e.g. derived from training samples or higher level constrains like a grammar, or given by a fix constant, e.g. $\frac{1}{N(u)}$. Thus the current value of $P(u_i|\mathbf{x})$ only depends on $P(\mathbf{x}|u_i)$.

In the here presented work, u_i is represented by its corresponding parametric Hidden Markov Model given by

$$M_{u_i} = \{S_{u_i}, V_{u_i}, A_{u_i}, B_{u_i}, \pi_{u_i}\} \tag{5.6}$$

with the set of states $S_{u_i} = \{s_1, s_2, s_3, \ldots, s_n\}$, the set of observations $V_{u_i} = \{v_1, v_2, v_3, \ldots, v_m\}$, the state transition probability matrix $A_{u_i} \in \mathbb{R}^{n \times n}$, the observation probability matrix $B_{u_i} \in \mathbb{R}^{n \times m}$ and the initial state distribution $\pi_{u_i} \in \mathbb{R}^n$.

It is assumed that the direct estimation of the joint conditional probability given an input frame sequences $\mathbf{x}$ and a representation u_i of the *i-th* unit $P(x_1, x_2, \ldots |u_i)$ is not feasible based on the training set only.

Therefore it is assumed, that the sequence of frame representations of a unit u_i, given an input sequence $\mathbf{x}$ can be generated by the Markov Model M_{u_i}, and that the joint probability that is generated by the model M_{u_i} moving through the set of state.

The produces a sequences of states $\mathscr{S}=(\mathbf{S}(x_t))_{t=1,\dots,T}$ with the mapping:

$$\mathbf{S}:\mathbf{x}\rightarrow S_{u_i},\mathbf{S}(x_i)=s_i. \tag{5.7}$$

In case of the here used HTK, the initial start state of each HMM is always the first state of the state sequence S_{u_i}. Therefore, the initial state distribution π_{u_i} of each unit is defined as $\pi_1 = P(\mathbf{S}(x_i)=s_1)=1$ and $\pi_i = P(\mathbf{S}(x_t)=s_1)=0$ for $i>1$.

The joint probability that the sequence $\mathscr{S}$ can be generated by the Markov Model M_{u_i} given an input sequence $\mathbf{x}$ can be calculated as the product of transition probabilities A and observation probabilities B_{u_i},

$$P(\mathbf{x},\mathscr{S}|M_{u_i}) = a_{12}b_1(x_1)a_{23}b_2(x_2)a_{32}b_3(x_3)\dots\ , \tag{5.8}$$

whereas the transition probability from state s_i to state $s_j \forall s_i, s_j \in S_{u_i}$ is defined by $a_{ij} := a_{(\mathbf{S}(x_i),\mathbf{S}(x_j))}, a_{ij} \in A_{u_i}$ and the observation probability of a state $\mathbf{S}(x_i)$ is defined by $b_i := b_{(\mathbf{S}(x_i))}, b_i \in B$

We assume that $P(\mathbf{x}|M_{u_i})$ corresponds to $P(\mathbf{x},\mathscr{S}|M_{u_i})$ by choosing for the sequence $\hat{\mathscr{S}}$ the one that maximizes $P(\mathbf{x},\mathscr{S}|M_{u_i})$

$$\hat{\mathscr{S}} = \underset{\mathscr{S}}{\operatorname{argmax}}\left(a_{12}\prod_{t=1}^{T}a_{(t,t+1)}b_t(x_t)\right)\ , \tag{5.9}$$

and the probability follows by

$$P(\mathbf{x}|M_{u_i}) = P(\mathbf{x},\hat{\mathscr{S}}|M_{u_i})\ . \tag{5.10}$$

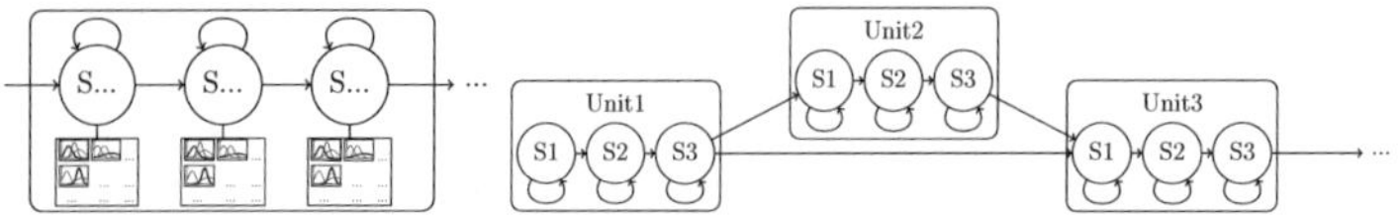

Figure 5.1.: Visual representation of an action unit and their concatenation by transition.

This leads back to the idea that the model M_{u_i} is a representation of the given unit u_i and that the best path through M_{u_i} corresponds to the probability $P(\mathbf{x}|u_i)$ of the observation of a unit u_i given an input sequence $\mathbf{x}$

$$P(\mathbf{x}|u_i) = P(\mathbf{x}|M_{u_i}) \; . \tag{5.11}$$

The observation probability is modeled in form of Gaussian mixture models defined as

$$b_j(x_t) = \sum_{k=1}^{K} \pi_k N(x_t; \mu_k, \sigma_k) \tag{5.12}$$

with

$$N(\mathbf{x}; \mu, \sigma) = \frac{1}{\sqrt{(2\pi)^n |\sigma|}} e^{-\frac{1}{2}(x-\mu)^T \sigma^{-1} (x-\mu)} \; , \tag{5.13}$$

where n is the dimension of the input sequence $\mathbf{x}$, μ the n-dimensional mean vector, σ the $n \times n$ covariance matrix and $|\sigma|$ the determinant of σ .

The HMMs are initialized by dividing the training sequences equally among the predefined number of states. The initial Gaussian components are computed from the training samples. The HMMs are defined to follow a left-to-right feed forward topology, allowing only self-transitions and transitions to the next state. The related transition probability matrix is always an upper bidiagonal matrix with non-zero entries along the main diagonal (self-transitions) and the diagonal above (transitions to the next state). The initial transition probability matrix is defined by

$$a_{ij} = \begin{cases} 0, & i > j, j > i+1, \\ a_{self}, & i = j, \\ a_{trans}, & i = j+1. \end{cases} , \quad (5.14)$$

with the default values for $a_{self} = 0.7$ and $a_{trans} = 0.3$. The initial values have been determined heuristically by parameter search on sample data. The transitions from the start and end state are treated separately by setting the start state transition to $a_{12} = 1$ and any other $a_{1j} = 0, j \neq 2$ and the end state transition to $a_{nn} = 0$ The parameters A and B of the HMM are optimized using Baum-Welch reestimation. An example of the HTK notation of a trained HMM is shown in appendix A. For the decoding of HMMs the Viterbi algorithm is used, computing the probability $\psi_{\mathbf{S}(x_t)}(t)$ for the best path from state i to state j at time t given an input sequence by summing up log transition probabilities and log output probabilities as defined by

$$\psi_{\mathbf{S}(x_t)}(t) = \max_j \Big(\psi_{\mathbf{S}(x_{(t-1)})}(t-1) + log(a_{ij}) + log(b_j(x_t)) \Big) . \quad (5.15)$$

5.3. Modeling of Action Sequences

As the recognition of simple units can be seen as a first step to analyze ongoing motion, it is unusual and a rather artificial assumption that everyday task consist of only one small action unit. It is more likely that everyday activities are made up from a set of action units, and of course, that units generating meaningful tasks are not executed at random. Therefore, tasks can be defined as combinations of action units. This concept has some advantages compared to the concept of treating a complete task at a time. First, breaking down the complete tasks into smaller units allows not only the recognition of the task as a whole, but also the parsing of included action units, their execution order leading to a more detailed representation and segmentation of the input sequence. Second, the bottom up construc-

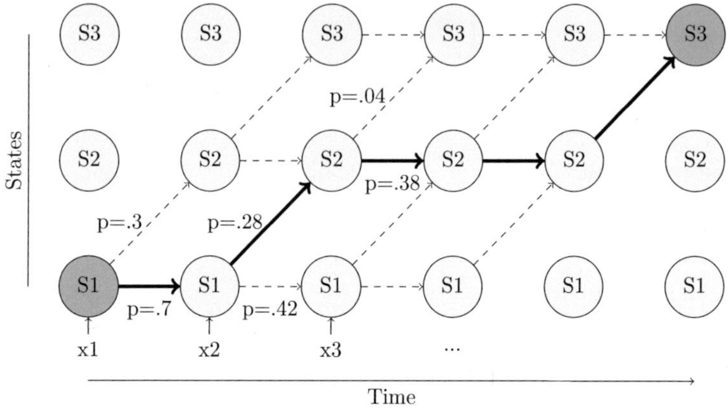

Figure 5.2.: Example for state transition in a three-state left-to-right HMM

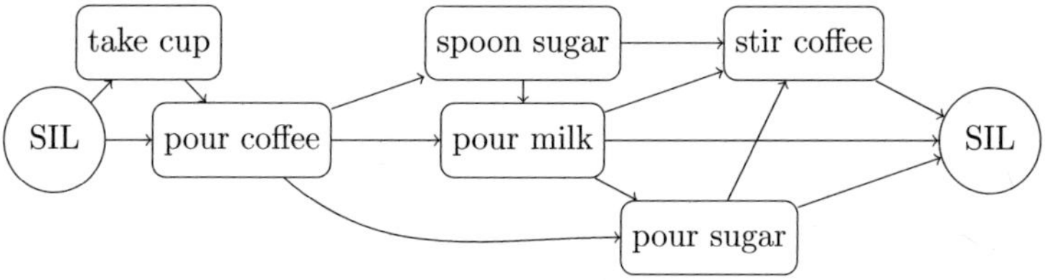

Figure 5.3.: Example for the transition between different units within a sequences for the activity "making coffee"

tion of tasks from single independent units allows a higher flexibility in terms of dealing with unknown combinations of units up to the recognition of new, unseen tasks.

In this work possible combinations of units are defined by a context-free grammar. The choice of a context free grammar is based on theoretical and practical considerations. On the theoretical side, a context free grammar is the least powerful grammar to defining recursive structures and specific counts of terminals as they arise in context of human actions. On the practical side, the specification of production rules based on context free grammars is supported by the here used HTK framework.

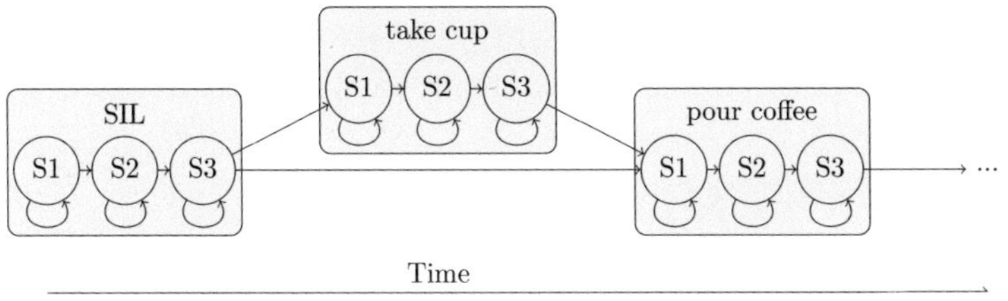

Figure 5.4.: Concatenation of action units on the level of HMM states. Begin and end states are the entrance resp. exit points for each unit.

The recognition of sequences is based on the token passing concept for connected speech recognition (see [YEG$^+$06] chp. 13.1, [YRT89]), augmenting the partial log probability $\psi_{S_X}(t)$ with word link records, or in the here presented case, unit link records describing the transition from one unit to the next. To compute the most probably sequence again the Viterbi algorithm is used (see equ. 5.15). At any time t , the link records can be traced back to get the current most probable path, meaning the most probable combination of units, and the position of the unit boundaries, meaning the segmentation of the sequences until time t.

5.3.1. Relation of Feature Dimensions and Number of Mixtures

A point that differs the here presented approach of standard speech recognition is beside the formulation of different units and action grammars the structure of input features. As the number of states as well as the number of used Gaussian mixtures is critical for recognition, they are evaluated by cross validation on the training set. Some examples of the evaluation of combinations of states and mixtures is discussed in the following.

To evaluate the best parameter configuration, the number of Gaussian mixtures has been varied from 1 up to 15 mixtures. No matter the number of states, recognition results tend to be better for low number of mixtures (see Fig. 5.8, p. 127). This lets conclude that a higher number of mixtures tends to overfit the training data. It can be assumed that the effect is based on high dimensionality of the data given relatively few training samples. This effect becomes clearer, the more dimensions are used to represent the frame signature.

On can see that a low dimensional input, resp. a small number of clusters, have a low sparsity level, but a high separation level, whereas higher dimensional input has a high sparsity but low separability by Gaussian mixtures.

5.3.2. Modeling of Temporal Distribution by Variable Number of States

The second difference of the given video representation is the high variability in the duration of different units compared to spoken phonemes. Units, e.g. of the ADL dataset (see 5.9, p. 128), can vary from 20 frames to over 200 frames. As for datasets with low variability, one fixed number of states works for all features, it is necessary for datasets with highly variable units to adapt the number of states s_n of a set of state S_{u_i} of a unit u_i according to unit length. To do this, different methods have been evaluated. First is an exponential mapping of mean feature length to the number of states, second would be a linear mapping.

To compute the mean length of the unit u_i, the mean of the length of the training data $\mathbf{X}_{u_i} = \{\mathbf{x}_1, \mathbf{x}_2, \mathbf{x}_3, \ldots, \mathbf{x}_N\}$ with corresponding length $T_1, T_2, T_3, \ldots, T_N$ is considered.

The exponential mapping would use the rounded square root of the mean number of frames as number of states whereas a linear mapping keeps a fixed factor for the number of states for each unit u_i as can be seen in equ. 5.16 and equ. 5.17.

$$m_{exp}(u_i) = \sqrt{\frac{1}{N}\sum_{n=1}^{N} T_n}\,, \tag{5.16}$$

$$m_{lin}(u_i) = a_{lin}\frac{1}{N}\sum_{n=1}^{N} T_n\,. \tag{5.17}$$

The evaluation shows that the adaptive modeling of states, exponential and adaptive modeling, usually works better than a fixed number of states. Further, a linear model seems to give a better representation of each unit than an exponential mapping.

5.4. Evaluation of Temporal Modeling

Different aspects of the proposed approach have been evaluated. The following section deals with the temporal modeling of activities and the advantage of semantic parsing. Therefore, similar to the previous chapter, HOGHOF as well as flow features are used to train the presented system and the output of the recognizer is compared to the results of SVM classification. To evaluate the performance of temporal recognition results are reported for each frame as well as for complete action sequences. Further the unit recognition, representing the inner structure of an action, is analyzed by applying different metrics like accuracy after DTW and word accuracy rate.

The proposed method has been evaluate on three different datasets namely the BKT dataset, the ADL dataset and the breakfast dataset, all varying in size, complexity and structure. As the BTK dataset, as the simplest of all, just shows staged actors with repetitive movements, the breakfast dataset comprises data records of 52 people working in real kitchens without any further constrains. Considering the size of the different dataset, there are about 150 clips in the ADL dataset and almost 2000 clips available for the breakfast dataset.

5.4.1. Reference System Description

For the here proposed work, the speech recognition toolbox HTK [YEG$^+$06] has been adapted for the case of temporal activity analysis.

It is assumed that for each dataset, a frame based feature representation is available. Further, to allow training and evaluation of action units, a frame-based segmentation of the data is needed, assigning each frame to its respective action unit. In case of the here used datasets, the labeling is done by hand, but it is pointed out that also automatically or semi-automatically segmentation techniques might be applied for future approaches.

The evaluation has been done on the proposed flow features and compared to the performance of the HOGHOF feature descriptors on the same system setup. Additionally, the results are compared to the recognition accuracy of a standard discriminative classification as reported in Sec. 4.5.2.

Training stage

For the training stage, a dictionary is built of all available action units. Each element in the dictionary is represented by an HMM in the final action model.

For the training of HMMs, an initial HMM is built for each action unit, defining the number of states, the topology, e.g. in this case strict forward left-to-right, the initial transition probabilities with $a_{self} = 0.6$ and $a_{trans} = 0.4$ and the number of Gaussians per state. In case of the here proposed work, the number of stages has is determined by cross validation, testing HMMs with fixed stages as well as with an adaptive number of stages depending on the mean frame length of the related unit. The number of stages in this case is either predefined as proposed by Schiel [Sch97] or determined by linear or logarithmic scaling. Additionally, the number of Gaussians has been evaluated. The defined parameters are globally optimized and constant for all HMMs.

The HMMs are trained by using the training samples of the related action unit. If there are too few units available, a random oversampling with additional Gaussian noise is used to generate a minimum of training samples.

After the training, the related models for all action units are stored in an action model and used for further recognition.

Recognition stage

For the recognition and parsing of complete sequences a grammar has to be built. The grammar notation used by HTK is based on the extended Backus-

Naur Form (EBNF) (see ISO/IEC 14977 standard [Sta96]) and can be used used to specify the order of units. For the here presented work the grammar for the BKT and the ADL dataset has be specified by hand in a top-down process. For the Breakfast dataset, this has shown unfeasible because of the complexity and variation of action sequences. Here the grammar has been built in an automatically bottom up process by parsing and encoding all possible paths from the full dataset. A listing of the grammars of the BKT and ADL dataset, as well an excerpt of the grammar of the Breakfast dataset is given in appendix B.

The grammar file is compiled into a Standard Lattice Format word network and subsequently used to drive the recognition process. For the recognition of unknown sequences, the probability of any path through the network is computed and the most likely path is given as recognition output. For the path search HTK uses a combination of token passing and different pruning strategies, keeping only the n-best hypothesis for the current time step. The transcription of the most likely path is written to the output file containing start and end time of each action unit and its total log probability. The related sequence label is determined by matching the written output to the related grammar.

5.4.2. Evaluation Criteria

As the focus of the proposed approach is on the recognition of the temporal analysis of video content and the segmentation of the ongoing video, the evaluation also focuses on those specific aspects of the recognition system. The resulting output is analyzed in terms of units and unit boundaries. As the number of resulting units is not necessarily consistent with the number of annotated units a direct one-to-one matching is not always feasible in this context. Therefore, different methods for error measurement are discussed and used for the evaluation.

Corresponding to the standard evaluation procedure for action recognition, an additional evaluation criterion is the overall activity recognition accuracy.

Unit Recognition

To compare the output of the unit recognition to the reference sequence, different techniques and metrics are considered. In case of frame based error computation, a simple one-to-one frame matching can be applied, as reference and recognized sequence have the same amount of frames. To compare the recognized action units to the labeling of the reference sequence, one has to remark that the number of resulting units of a sequences does not necessary match the number of units of the reference sequences. Therefore, a sequence alignment of the recognized sequence to the reference sequence is done as a preprocessing step. For sequence alignment, different strategies based on local or global optimization can be applied. In the following evaluation dynamic time warping (DTW) is used to calculate the alignment between the two given sequences. Three different types of errors can occur during the recognition process:

- Misclassifications arise when a unit is assigned to the wrong class. $unit_{miss}$ refers to the number of all misclassified units in a sequence.
- Insertions arise when a unit is recognized and inserted that has not been annotated. $unit_{ins}$ refers to the number of all insertions in a sequence.
- Deletions arise when units are omitted that have been originally labeled in the ground truth. $unit_{del}$ refers to the number of all deletions in a sequence.

An example for an insertion error is given in Fig. 5.5. Here five units have been recognized, but the original video only consists of four different units. For the frame-based error computation, all falsely labeled frames have been

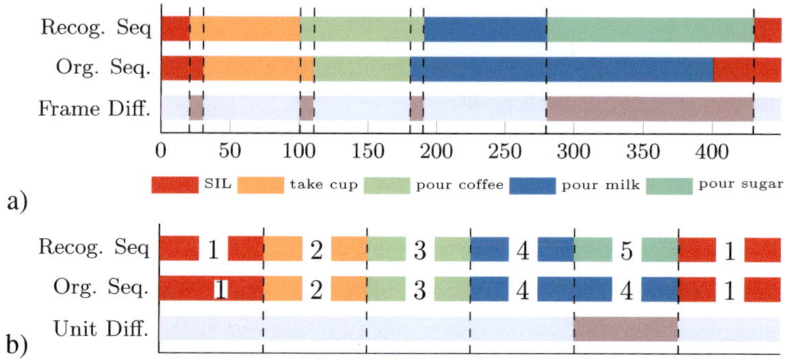

Figure 5.5.: Comparison between the original reference sequence and the predicted sequence with a) showing the frame-based comparison and b) the unit comparison

considered. For the unit error, it is obvious that unit (5) has been inserted and one insertion error is counted for this sequence.

Sequence parsing accuracy

The most relaxed measurement is to compare the aligned sequences with respect to units that are not correctly classified. Thus, all falsely recognized units are considered without distinguishing insertions, deletions or misclassification. Further, counting errors arising if more or less entities of the same unit appearing in a row are falsely counted are omitted for example when the test person is cutting five times in a row and only three times are recognized. The exact count of repetitions is not taken into account by this method. Instead, it provides a measure for the accuracy of the overall sequence parsing by

$$A_{par} = \frac{unit_{corr}}{unit_{all}} \tag{5.18}$$

with $unit_{corr}$ referring to the number all correctly classified units in the sequence and $unit_{all}$ referring to the number of all units after DTW, including misclassifications and insertions.

Unit accuracy and hit rate

A more restrictive measurement, the unit accuracy, considers similar to word accuracy in speech recognition the number of false units relative to the number of originally labeled units. To compute the unit accuracy, three different types of errors are considered: the unit insertions, deletions, and the misclassified units. The unit accuracy is computed parallel to the word accuracy by taking the number of original units $unit_{org}$ and subtracting all error counts, normalized by the number of original units, by

$$A_{unit_{acc}} = \frac{unit_{org} - unit_{miss} - unit_{ins} - unit_{del}}{unit_{org}} . \tag{5.19}$$

One has to remark that the unit accuracy, contrary to the other measurements used in this work, is defined by the interval of $]-\infty, 1]$. Thus, it can also take on negative values as the number of insertion errors $unit_{ins}$ is not limited and the sum of all three errors can become larger than the number of original units. To overcome this problem, the results will be reported by indicating the hit rate with reference to the overall count of resulting units

$$A_{unit_{hit}} = 1 - \frac{unit_{miss} + unit_{ins} + unit_{del}}{unit_{corr} + unit_{miss} + unit_{ins} + unit_{del}} . \tag{5.20}$$

The hit rate can be close to the overall sequence parsing accuracy, with the difference that the number of repetition of cyclic units is taken into account. If someone is cutting three times in a row but five 'cut' units are recognized, two insertion errors are counted. The difference will become visible especially in Sec. 5.4.4, where the influence of counting cyclic units will be discussed in more detail.

Frame based segmentation accuracy

To estimate the correct segmentation of the given sequence, it is considered how many frames the detected boundary deviates from the original labeling. Therefore the number of frames that were not labeled correctly is taken into account and the frame based accuracy is computed with resp. to the overall number frames in the reference sequence by

$$A_{seg} = \frac{frame_{corr}}{frame_{all}} . \tag{5.21}$$

Sequence Recognition

For the case of temporal recognition, the output is not a single class label, but the most probably combination of action units. Here, the class label is determined by matching the resulting unit sequence to its corresponding path as defined in the grammar. As each path is assigned to its respective sequence, the resulting class is given be the sequence the path origins from. To compute the recognition accuracy, the correct recognized activities act_{corr} are compared to the overall number of sequences act_{all}

$$A_{activity} = \frac{act_{corr}}{act_{all}} . \tag{5.22}$$

One has to remark that, even if the sequence of units is only partly correct, it will be counted as correctly recognized as long as its respective path belongs to the correct sequence class.

5.4.3. Evaluation of ADL Dataset

First, the ADL dataset is evaluated. One has to remark that this dataset is with only 15 clips per activity the smallest of the three datasets. It is thus an interesting example, as the number of samples for cross-validation and training is very low and thus a challenging example for a generative recognition model. Following the procedure presented in Sec. 4.5, the evaluation has been done for flow features and HOGHOF features as a state-of-the-art reference for feature descriptors.

Unit Recognition

First, the sequence parsing accuracy has been taken into account, counting the overall amount of correctly classified units. One can see from the results listed in Tab. 5.1 that the proposed flow features with a best accuracy of 64.15% clearly outperform HOGHOF features with 58.56% by ∼6%. Additionally, the standard deviation of the recognition accuracy considering the different cluster sizes is with 0.7% relatively small compared the standard deviation of HOGHOF features with 5.8% which shows that the proposed features are able to represent the overall unit activity in a robust manner.

Looking further at the results of the unit hit rate in Tab. 5.2, one can see that the overall result vary only by ∼2% from the sequences parsing accuracy. Here the influence of counting the overall amount of especially cyclic units becomes clear. To allow a more detailed discussion of this problem, Tab. 5.3 lists the mean insertion, deletion, and misclassification error per unit for the different cluster sizes. One can see that for HOGHOF features the overall error mainly results from insertions and misclassifications, whereas the error distribution of flow features is rather constant across the three error classes. Additional to the unit recognition, also the frame based recognition has been taken into account. The results in Tab. 5.4 show that here again, the proposed flow features perform with 52.36%

ADL dataset				
Sequence parsing accuracy				
cluster:	c30	c50	c100	c200
HOGHOF	**58.56**%	57.48%	52.33%	45.84%
cluster:	c30	c50	c100	c200
Flow features	64.03%	63.15%	**64.15**%	62.68%

Table 5.1.: Evaluation of sequence parsing accuracy with HTK using HOGHOF and flow features

ADL dataset				
Unit hit rate				
cluster:	c30	c50	c100	c200
HOGHOF	**56.49**%	55.89%	50.20%	44.47%
cluster:	c30	c50	c100	c200
Flow features	**62.38**%	61.53%	61.93%	60.44%

Table 5.2.: Evaluation of unit hit rate with HTK using HOGHOF and flow features

ADL dataset				
Unit insertion, deletion, and misclassification rate				
HOGHOF				
cluster:	c30	c50	c100	c200
insertion	0.8	2.7	2.4	2.0
deletion	1.2	0.6	0.8	1.2
misclassification	1.8	2.1	2.3	2.6
Flow features				
cluster:	c30	c50	c100	c200
insertion	0.9	1.0	1.8	1.5
deletion	1.2	1.0	0.7	1.0
misclassification	1.5	1.7	1.7	1.8

Table 5.3.: Evaluation of recognition with HTK for unit parsing using HOGHOF and flow features

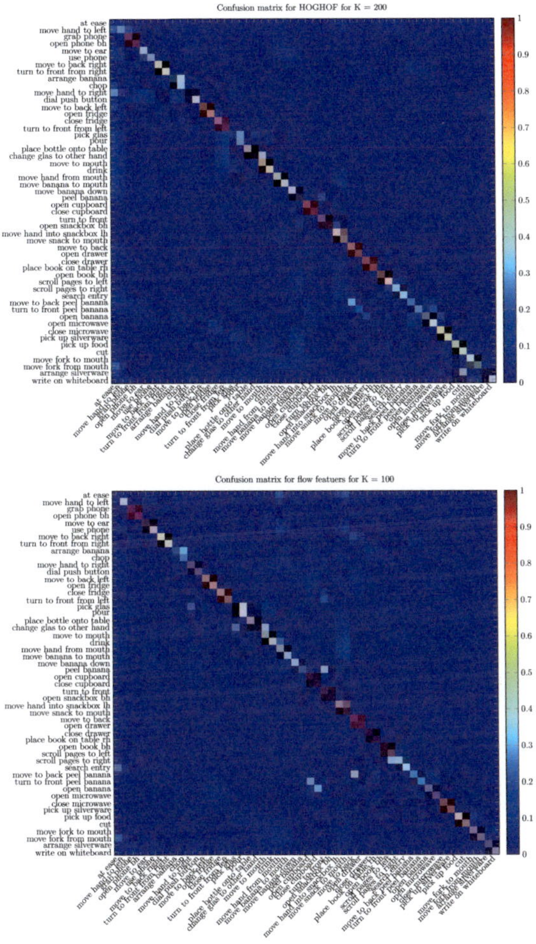

Figure 5.6.: Confusion matrix of the recognition accuracy for units per frame based on HOGHOF and flow features. One can see that optional units have only few occurrences (see Fig. 5.7), leading to low recognition accuracy because they are not enforced by grammar.

ADL dataset					
Frame based accuracy					
cluster:	c30	c50	c100	c200	c2000
HOGHOF	**45.69%**	43.85%	38.37%	33.17%	-
best discr. acc.	*17.43%*	*18.77%*	*21.16%*	*20.49%*	*21.75%*
cluster:	c30	c50	c100	c200	c2000
Flow features	49.97%	49.88%	**52.36%**	49.72%	-
best discr. acc.	*23.20%*	*25.81%*	*25.67%*	*26.09%*	*29.41%*

Table 5.4.: Evaluation of frame based unit classification accuracy with HTK using HOGHOF and flow features

better than the reference HOGHOF features with 45.69%. Overall, this is an improvement of more than 20% compared to the results of the discriminative classification with 29.41% for flow features and 21.75% HOGHOF recognition accuracy as seen in Sec. 4.5 (p. 81). One can see that the temporal modeling leads to almost a doubling of the original recognition accuracy. Having a closer look at the recognition of single units in Fig. 5.6, one can see that half of the units were recognized with an accuracy of 60% resp. 73% or better. Thus instead of recognizing a few units reliably, 67.3% of all units show recognition rates above 50% with only ∼5% of units that show recognition rates below 10%. Considering the units with low recognition rates, e.g. "open snackbox", "arrange banana" or "pick glass", one can see they share two characteristics: First, they are usually optional units in the overall grammar and related to this, they usually provide fewer training samples as mandatory units as can be seen in Fig. 5.7. Second, they are not enforced by the grammar itself and thus, as can be seen in the related confusion matrix, often merge with neighbored units. This effect is equally visible for both type of features and can therefore rather be attributed to the recognition framework than to the feature descriptor themselves. Additional to the overall recognition performance, the training properties of the recognition framework have been taken into account. As mentioned in Sec. 5.4.1, for each dataset the optimal number of states of the HMM as well

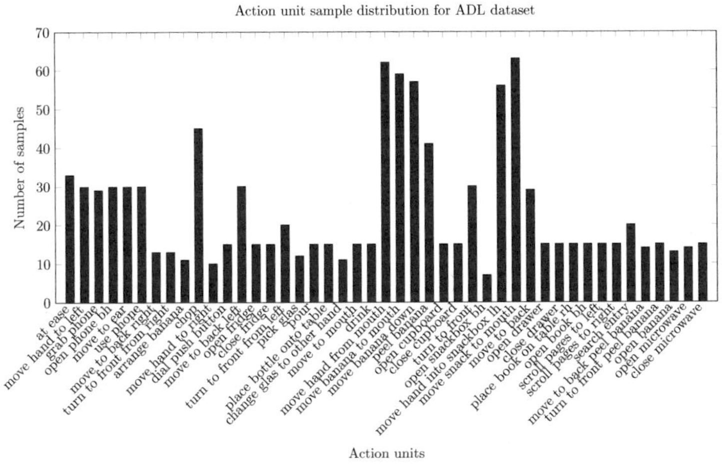

Figure 5.7.: Distribution of number of samples per action unit.

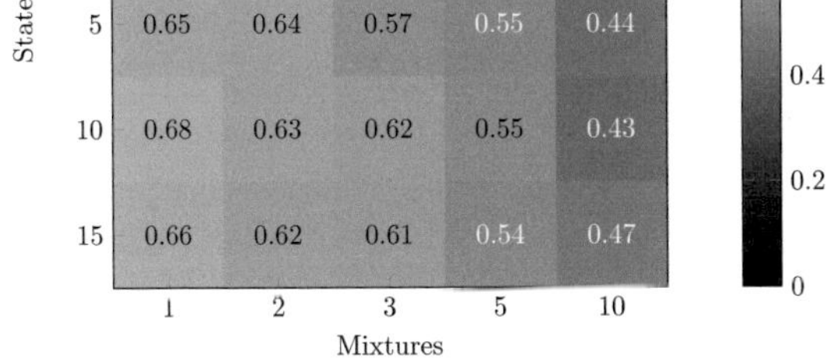

Figure 5.8.: Mean results for parameter search by cross validation. One can see that Gaussian mixture models with only few mixtures perform generally better, as well as HMMs with a either an adaptive number of states or a fixed larger number of states.

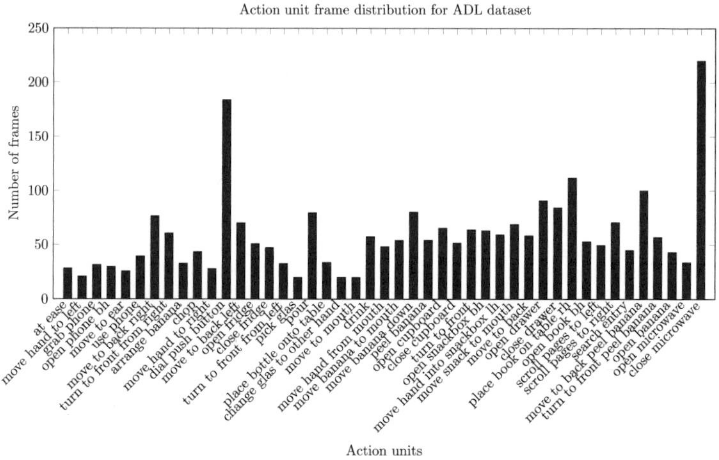

Figure 5.9.: Mean number of frames per unit

as the number of Gaussian mixtures per state has be determined by cross validation. As the proposed system has not been evaluated by others so far, and there are no comparable empirical values, the training comprises a larger parameter space testing for 1, 2, 3, 5 and 10 Gaussian mixtures and 5, 10 and 15 states, adaptive number of states and linear scaling of mean unit length. The results of the grid search over all 5 splits are shown in Fig. 5.8. One can see that fewer numbers of mixtures usually perform better than a larger number of mixtures. This can be an indication that, given the high dimensional space, a larger number of mixtures might lead to an over-fitting of the relatively few training samples whereas fewer mixtures better approximate the overall data distribution. Looking at the number of states, one can see that for this dataset, an adaptive number of states produces slightly better results than a fix number of 10 states. Overall linear scaling by factor 10 produces the worst results. This can be explained by looking at the mean number of frames per unit as shown in Fig. 5.9 showing that almost half of the units have a mean duration of less than 50 frames. Thus, the resulting number of states will fall below 5 states when linear scaling is applied and therefore also produce worse results than fixed number of states.

Sequence Recognition

Looking at the sequence recognition in Tab. 5.5, one can see flow features in combination with temporal modeling outperform the reference descriptor. Especially for the activities "answer phone", "eat snack" and "lookup in phonebook" they score a perfect 100% (see Fig. 5.10). The only major confusion is in case of "eat snack" and "peel banana" as in both cases there is mainly a repetitive up and down motion in the sequences and thus, the overall flow pattern becomes quiet similar.

ADL dataset					
Sequence accuracy					
cluster:	c30	c50	c100	c200	c2000
HOGHOF	71.33%	68.89%	60.67%	50.67%	-
best discr. acc.	*66.67%*	*71.33%*	*76.67%*	*81.33%*	*86.67%*
cluster:	c30	c50	c100	c200	c2000
Flow features	74.00%	74.00%	76.00%	75.33%	-
best discr. acc.	*66.00%*	*69.33%*	*76.00%*	*74.67%*	*76.00%*

Table 5.5.: Evaluation of sequences recognition with HTK using HOGHOF and flow features

But one has also to remark that the overall accuracy of the temporal recognition system is below the best accuracy achieved by discriminative classifiers, performing at best at 76.0% whereas the best discriminative result is reached by HOGHOF features with 86.67%. The drop in overall sequence recognition accuracy reveals in this case one of the drawbacks of generative modeling, namely the need for enough training data. As discriminative models are built to easily generalize from few examples to a large range of samples, generative models are only based on the available training data. When there are only few training samples, especially the underlying Gaussian mixtures might not be able to capture all possible variations that

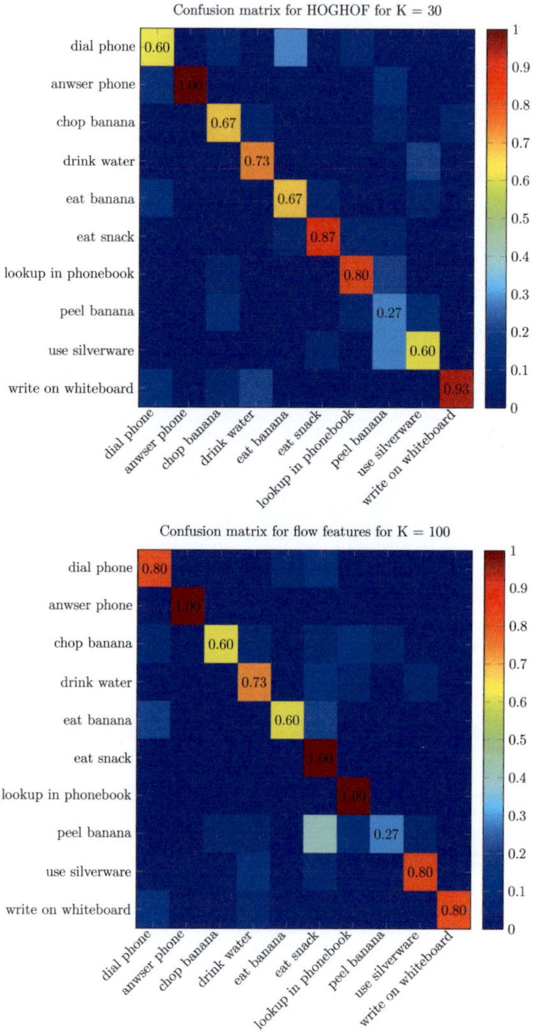

Figure 5.10.: Confusion matrix of the recognition accuracy of sequences based on HOGHOF and flow features

arise in the test data. Additionally, few samples of high dimensional input data with a lot of variations may result in degenerated models and thus only give a sub-optimal sequence recognition accuracy.

Another point to consider in this context is that discriminative models encode the features of the complete sequences in one histogram. This also includes, in case of HOGHOF, knowledge about specific object appearances in certain sequences, e.g. a book in "lookup in phone book". Thus it is not possible to determine how far the overall recognition is based on object or motion information. But it can be shown in context of the following two datasets that, if the object information diminishes, e.g. because of the size of the object or becomes unspecific when the shape and appearance changes, the proposed model is able to outperform discriminative approaches.

Overall the evaluation of the ADL dataset shows, that the recognition accuracy can drop in case of full sequence recognition compared to the results reached by discriminative classification but in case of unit classification (see Sec. 4.5.3, Tab. 4.6 and Tab. 4.5) clearly outperforms discriminative classifiers. This can be seen a first hint for the performance of the proposed system when it comes to the semantic analysis of video data.

5.4.4. Evaluation of BKT Dataset

The second evaluated dataset is the BKT dataset. The dataset mainly provides more samples per activity, executed by only one test persons, and has fewer variations in terms of execution order than the other two evaluated datasets. It can be seen as a good example for generative modeling of activities as it provides enough samples with only few variations.

For the evaluation of sequence recognition with temporal modeling both feature types, HOGHOF and the here proposed flow features are considered and the evaluation is again done for cluster sizes of 30, 50, 100 and 200 dimensions.

Unit Recognition

In terms of unit classification the temporal modeling is outperforming discriminative classification. But, as there are only two activity misclassifications overall, it might be difficult to draw any reliable conclusion out of recognition performance only.

Therefore, the first evaluation is based on the absolute numbers of recognized units: for HOGHOF features, the system outputs an overall of 1414 units of 1591 units to recognize. This is a drop of 177 units compared to the original labels and shows that here, some cyclic activities have not been counted correctly. An example for the miscount is e.g. given when three stirring units were performed in the video, but only two are recognized in the resulting sequence. After aligning the resulting units with the original labels by DTW, one gets 1388 unit correctly labeled units and 203 wrong ones. Looking at the resulting confusion matrix for the frame based evaluation, one can see that the main issue arising in this context, beside the two falsely classified sequences, is mainly the transition between the single units. This corresponds to the observation of missed cyclic intervals as here also, the main factor is the determination of the right segment border between two cycles.

For flow features, one can observe contrary characteristics: here the overall output are 1660 units where only 1576 units were labeled, thus there are 84 insertions. But after aligning it shows that 1634 out of the 1660 units are correctly classified and 26 are wrong. Thus a larger fraction of the insertions are cyclic units that have been counted too often. This shows that here, the system is rather temporal oversegmentation the single units. This can also be seen by looking at the related confusion matrix which shows only few misclassified frames. This is a hint that the borders are usually determined correctly, but when looking at the overall number of units, for the price of oversegmenting the overall activities.

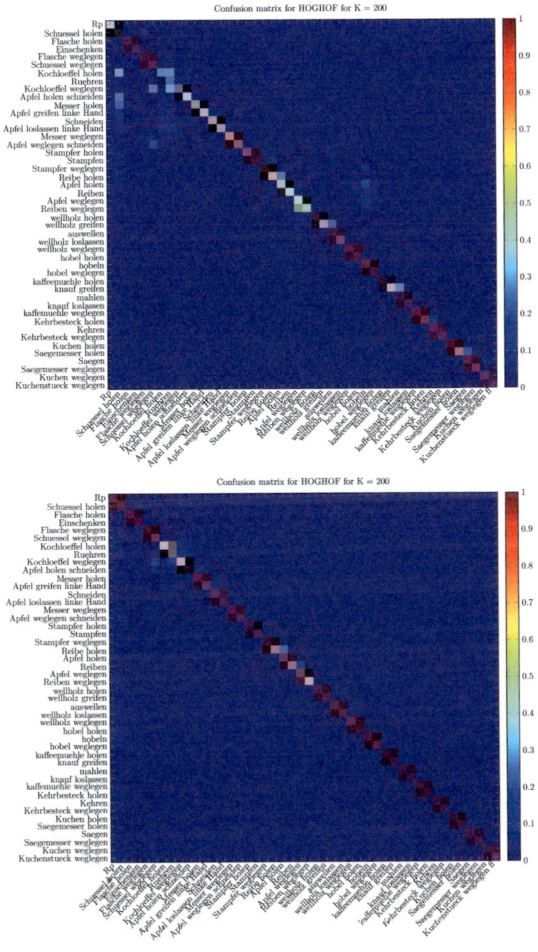

Figure 5.11.: Confusion matrix of the recognition accuracy for units per frame based on HOGHOF and flow features over 10 frames

BKT dataset				
Sequence parsing accuracy				
cluster:	c30	c50	c100	c200
HOGHOF	84.91%	88.15%	87.43%	89.71%
cluster:	c30	c50	c100	c200
Flow Features	98.40%	97.96%	98.06%	97.10%

Table 5.6.: Evaluation of the BKT unit classification rate with HTK using HOGHOF and flow features

BKT dataset				
Frame based accuracy				
cluster:	c30	c50	c100	c200
HOGHOF	81.78%	82.16%	81.12%	82.18%
best discr. acc.	*41.48%*	*44.71%*	*49.97%*	*54.00%*
cluster:	c30	c50	c100	c200
Flow features	91.43%	91.67%	91.81%	91.76%
best discr. acc.	*55.11%*	*58.56%*	*59.47%*	*59.11%*

Table 5.7.: Evaluation of recognition with HTK for frame based unit classification using HOGHOF and flow features

Another important point becomes clear when looking at the evaluation of the unit hit rate in Tab. 5.6, the frame based segmentation accuracy in Tab. 5.7 and the sequence accuracy in Tab 5.8 compared to discriminative classification as shown in Sec. 4.5.4 (p. 93).

Here the temporal modeling clearly outperforms the previously evaluated classifiers by more than 30% reaching a frame based segmentation accuracy of 91.92% compared to 59.47% reached by the discriminative approach (see. Tab 5.7). In absolute numbers, of overall 122,473 frames, the system based on HOGHOF classified 100,177 frames correct and 22,296 false, whereas the system based on flow features classified 115,570 correct and 10,846 false.

BKT dataset				
Sequence accuracy				
cluster:	c30	c50	c100	c200
HOGHOF	99.20%	99.20%	98.00%	97.20%
best discr. acc.	*99.57%*	*98.26%*	*100.00%*	*100.00%*
cluster:	c30	c50	c100	c200
Flow features	100.0%	99.60%	100.0%	100.0%
best discr. acc.	*94.00%*	*93.60%*	*95.20%*	*96.80%*

Table 5.8.: Evaluation of sequences recognition with HTK using HOGHOF and flow features

Sequence Recognition

One can see from Tab. 5.8 that the overall sequence recognition stays constant in case of HOGHOF features and rises for the case of flow features, reaching a recognition rate of 100% for 30, 50 and 100 cluster dimensions. This is consistent with the results of discriminative classification, showing that the recognition by temporal modeling can reach comparable results to state-of-the-art classifiers.

Thus, one has to remark that it is difficult to find a fair comparison on the level of unit recognition between two approaches, one has also to recognize that the here shown results in terms of unit recognition accuracy are so far unmatched by any other system.

5.4.5. Evaluation of Breakfast Dataset

As already seen in the first part of the evaluation (Sec. 4.5.5, p. 95), the Breakfast dataset might be the most challenging of the three datasets. Discriminative classification showed only poor results on this type of data, especially in terms of unit recognition (see Tab. 4.10, p. 98).

The following evaluation of the same data, based on a temporal modeling approach, shows the influence of temporal models by increasing the semantic parsing accuracy as well as overall recognition accuracy (see Tab. 5.14) in context of an increased data complexity.

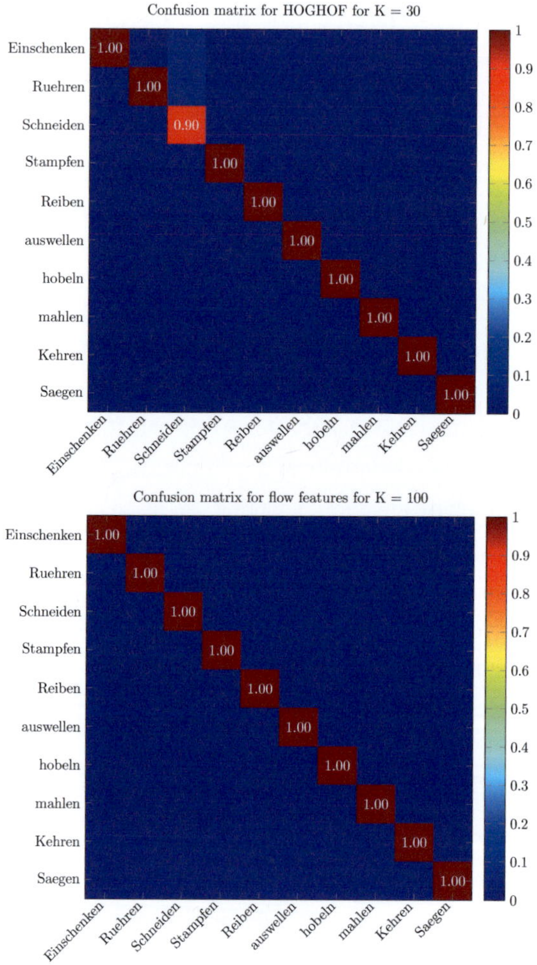

Figure 5.12.: Confusion matrix of the recognition accuracy for sequences based on HOGHOF and flow features

For the training, the parameter search regarding the optimal number of states and the optimal number of Gaussian mixtures has only been run ones for the example of HOGHOF features with $K = 30$ cluster. Different from the evaluation of the other two datasets, the results of parameter estimation for this dataset have shown to be unambiguous and have therefore been used in the following for all features and cluster sizes.

Unit Recognition

First, the unit recognition accuracy for the temporal modeling has been evaluated and compared to the results of discriminative classification. The advantage of temporal modeling becomes first visible when looking at the sequence parsing accuracy in Tab. 5.9 as well as on the frame based accuracy in Tab. 5.12. In case of sequence parsing accuracy HOGHOF features show with 31.83% a higher accuracy than flow features with 23.03%. This is a significant drop compared to the other two dataset. But, as sequence recognition shows (Tab. 5.14, p. 141) only $\sim 30\% - \sim 40\%$ of all sequences were recognized correctly. Considering the unit structure of this dataset, the unit recognition will usually not produce better results than the overall sequence recognition. To put this result in context of the other two evaluated dataset, Tab. 5.10 shows the results of the parsing accuracy of the correct recognized sequences only. Here it can be seen that, assuming the overall sequence was recognized correctly, the related units only deviate by a smaller portion form the original reference sequence. Additionally it becomes clear that the overall sequences parsing with $\sim$60% is comparable to the results of the other two datasets.

To be able to evaluate the influence of grammar, the same evaluation has been executed without a grammar, allowing transitions from each unit to the next one. The results are shown in Tab. 5.11. One can see that the omission of a higher level structure clearly reduces the overall sequence parsing accuracy, leading to a drop of $\sim$20% down to 12.54%. Nevertheless, those

Breakfast dataset				
Sequence parsing accuracy				
cluster:	c30	c50	c100	c200
HOGHOF	30.41%	**31.82%**	31.30%	31.70%
cluster:	c30	c50	c100	c200
Flow features	**23.03%**	21.65%	21.76%	21.51%

Table 5.9.: Evaluation of recognition accuracy with HTK for sequence parsing using HOGHOF and flow features

Breakfast dataset				
Sequence parsing accuracy of correct sequences only				
cluster:	c30	c50	c100	c200
HOGHOF	**58.5%**	57.5%	56.9%	57.6%
cluster:	c30	c50	c100	c200
Flow features	**56.8%**	56.4%	55.2%	56.7%

Table 5.10.: Evaluation of recognition with HTK for unit parsing using HOGHOF and flow features

Breakfast dataset				
Sequence parsing accuracy without grammar				
cluster:	c30	c50	c100	c200
HOGHOF	10.95%	11.89%	12.30%	12.54%
cluster:	c30	c50	c100	c200
Flow features	8.43%	8.79%	8.09%	9.20%

Table 5.11.: Evaluation of recognition with HTK for unit parsing without grammar using HOGHOF and flow features

Breakfast dataset				
Frame based accuracy				
cluster:	c30	c50	c100	c200
HOGHOF	**28.85%**	28.76%	26.57%	26.57%
best discr. acc.	*5.56%*	*5.68%*	*6.09%*	*6.40%*
cluster:	c30	c50	c100	c200
Flow features	24.46%	24.20%	22.48%	**24.50%**
best discr. acc.	*5.00%*	*5.52%*	*6.33%*	*5.65%*

Table 5.12.: Evaluation of recognition with HTK for frame based unit classification using HOGHOF and flow features

Breakfast dataset				
Frame based accuracy without grammar				
cluster:	c30	c50	c100	c200
HOGHOF	12.12%	12.08%	12.41%	11.96%
cluster:	c30	c50	c100	c200
Flow features	11.62%	12.00%	11.75%	13.23%

Table 5.13.: Evaluation of recognition with HTK for frame based unit classification using HOGHOF and flow features

results are still better than the results gained by discriminative classification ranging from 5% to 6% (see Tab. 5.12). It shows that not only the higher level semantic modeling plays an important role, but also that the low level temporal encoding given by the states of the single HMMs is a first, important step towards temporal encoding as, on this level, recognition results are still better than the ones gained by discriminative classification.

Looking at the confusion matrix for both feature types in Fig. 5.13, one can see that for both cases some units tend to get rather confused with others, namely those that can appear in different activities, e.g. "pour milk", but also units related to cutting fruits for fruit salad as "cut fruit", "put fruit to bowl" and "peel fruit". For the first category, the error mainly arises from false segmentation and parsing issues, which leads to the fact that units are confused with their neighbors. For the second category, the cutting of fruits,

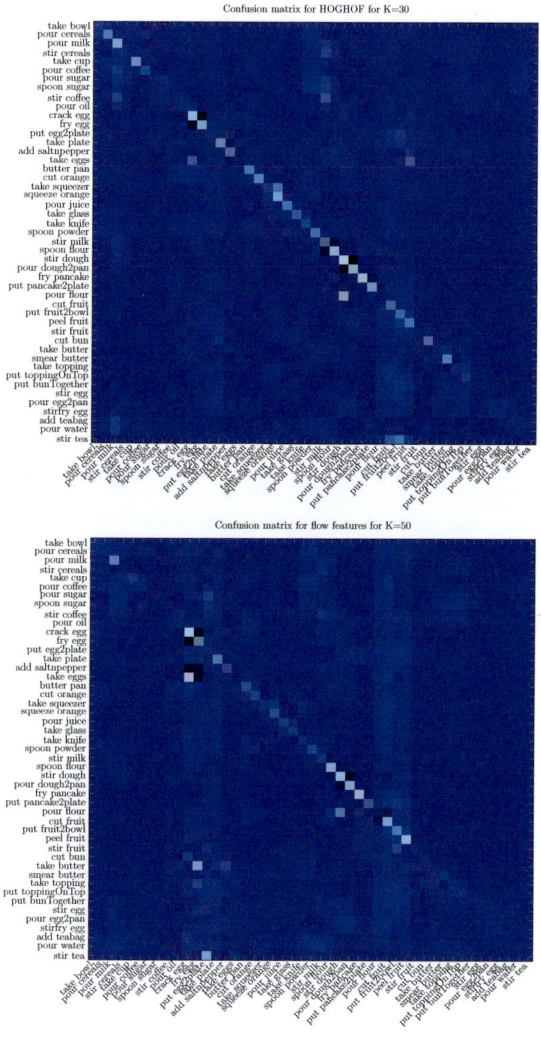

Figure 5.13.: Confusion matrix of the recognition accuracy for units per frame based on HOGHOF and flow features over 10 frames

Breakfast dataset				
Sequence accuracy				
cluster:	c30	c50	c100	c200
HOGHOF	38.46%	**40.53%**	38.91%	39.40%
best discr. acc.	*25.15%*	*26.04%*	*21.53%*	*21.03%*
cluster:	c30	c50	c100	c200
Flow features	**28.68%**	27.06%	26.69%	27.10%
best discr. acc.	*22.34%*	*21.74%*	*23.20%*	*26.00%*

Table 5.14.: Evaluation of sequences recognition with HTK using HOGHOF and flow features original videos and videos with unified viewpoint

the error results from falsely classified sequences. Here the cyclic nature of the cutting and peeling of different fruits results in a larger overall number of errors, as the units themselves can appear multiple times in one sequence what is not the case for acyclic units, e.g. "take bowl".

Sequence Recognition

In terms of sequences recognition the evaluation shows an increase of recognition accuracy compared to discriminative classification with HOG-HOF based recognition performing at best at 40.53% (+ 15.38%) and flow features with an accuracy of 28.68% (+ 2.68%). Looking at the related confusion matrix shown in Fig. 5.14, it can be seen that related activity groups, especially the preparation of drinks vs. food tend to be more confused among each other than with not related activities. This is based on two reasons: first, related activities share a higher number of similar units among each other. For example, three of five drink related activities start with the unit "take cup" and all of them include one or more units related to pouring or stirring. Second, the combination of HMMs and grammar implicitly encodes the possible length of a sequence. As HMMs require a sufficient number of frames for each state, grammars also define a minimum number of HMMs to pass through. Therefore, it is unlikely that very long activities like the preparation of pancakes get mixed up with very

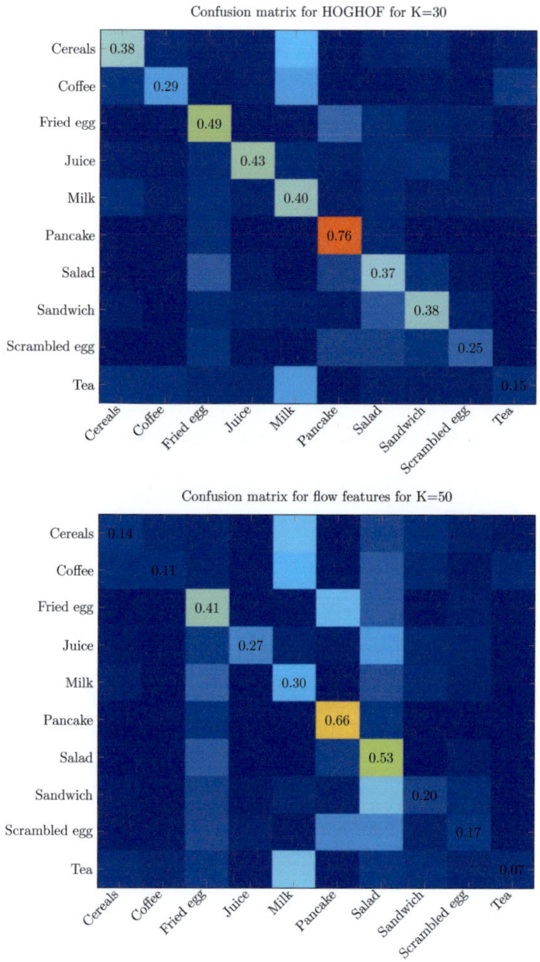

Figure 5.14.: Confusion matrix of the recognition accuracy for units per frame based on HOGHOF and flow features over 10 frames

short ones like "preparing coffee". The only exception in the grouping for food vs. drink is the preparation of cereals. Even though it does not fit the literal grouping, one has to notice that this activity shares more units with drink-related activities like stirring and pouring than with food-related ones.

Additionally, a trend towards longer activities becomes visible when looking at the best activity of the food and drink group, the preparation of pancake and chocolate milk. With the exception of juice, which is very different in terms of units, the preparation of pancake and chocolate milk are both the longest activities of their related groups. Especially drink related activities tend to get mixed up with the longer model of "chocolate milk". So in both cases, the short drink preparation tasks and the longer food preparation, longer activities are preferred over short ones.

Overall, the evaluation especially of this very complex and challenging dataset shows the improvement that can be gained by applying hierarchical temporal models in context of human action recognition. Additionally, it shows that the application of such models is not restricted to the limited conditions of a lab space with highly choreographed actions, but that they can also work with activities recorded 'in the wild' and not only keep up with state of the art discriminative methods, but even outperform them under such difficult conditions.

5.5. Conclusion

The chapter gave an example for the realization of a hierarchical temporal modeling in context of video based activity recognition. The implementation is based on the open source HTK framework for automatic speech recognition (see. [YEG$^+$06]).

The first section described how longer activities were split into small units and how those units can be modeled by HMMs. The modeling of action units is on the lowest level based on multivariate Gaussian mixture models, which represent the possible feature distribution for each state in the HMM and are used to compute the probability of an input vector, or frame, belonging to the related state of the HMM. The transitions of one state to another are models in a transition probability matrix, whereas in the here presented case, the HMM transitions are based on a strict feed forward topology. This means that only self-transitions or transitions to the next state are allowed. Thus, the related transition matrix is an upper bidiagonal matrix with non-zero entries along the main diagonal and the diagonal above.

The resulting units can be concatenated to longer sequences of meaningful activities. The concatenation is guided by a context free grammar, which can either be built by hand or, in case of larger dataset, automatically by parsing the related segmentation information of the dataset. The concatenation of sequences is based on the token passing concept for connected speech recognition.

The following evaluation of the proposed approach is done with regard to the different aspects of unit recognition and sequential parsing, comprising the analysis of frame based segmentation of a video as well as the correctness of the resulting sequence of units itself.

The evaluation is performed on three different datasets representing the distinct characteristics of different application scenarios, form a staged actor in a fixed environment to real live records of different people in different locations. It shows that the proposed approach outperforms discriminative classifiers in all cases when it comes to the frame based recognition of action units within a video sequence. Further it shows that also for sequences recognition state-of-the-art results can be reached and even be significantly exceed given enough training samples. This is especially the case for more complex activity sequences, like for the case of the Breakfast dataset, where discriminative models fail to capture the temporal characteristics that are needed for a good recognition result.

The achieved results demonstrate the benefits of this method in terms of recognition of single units and activities, as well as for the sequential parsing of videos streams.

6. Conclusion

This work showed an approach to realize the temporal and semantic parsing of human activities in video data by focusing on the role of action units and their combination in human action recognition.

To address this questions, a combination of new features as well as the application of techniques from speech recognition is proposed to realize a recognition of action units and their combinations in video sequences. The proposed features are based on basic optical flow information which is interpolated and concatenated over time to build a representation of the ongoing motion, the flow features. They are used for a frame wise encoding of the overall video.

Based on this representation, an open source speech recognition framework is adapted to allow a recognition of the video sequences on unit level as well as a recognition of the overall sequences. Therefore, possible combinations of units are defined by a context free grammar to guide the recognition process and to lead to the parsing of complex sequences.

This allowed beside action recognition the semantic evaluation of the video as well as a frame based segmentation. The performance of the proposed approach is evaluated on datasets with varying complexity dealing with the daily living activities like basic kitchen tasks or the preparation of breakfast items.

It shows that with a growing structural complexity, the proposed temporal approach is able to outperform discriminative state of the art methods and gives rise to the hope that, in future, this kind of systems might allow some interesting answers to open questions in this context.

The proposed combination of flow features and temporal modeling has been shown to not only allow the recognition of action sequences, but also to parse the ongoing action units at task level.

The main advantages but also the limitations and drawback of the proposed method will be discussed in the following

6.1. Limitations of the Proposed Approach

The proposed system shows good performance on the presented datasets, but there are also some drawbacks in this type of system.

The presented system relays on hand segmented training data on unit level, which requires a lot of time for the labeling and is not always available. Therefore, this kind of systems can become unfeasible when it comes to very large datasets for example in context of video indexing either because there is no segmented data or because the number of units themselves is unknown. There are two possible solutions in this case. First, in case of an existing, but small set of labeled units, a bootstrapping of the overall system might be feasible. In this case, the labeled units would be used for an initial training and the larger amount of training data would be used only in terms of a reestimation procedure to refine the original models. Second in case of no labeled training data at all, it might be thinkable to use automatic segmentation of the video data in combination with clustering to build the units in an unsupervised manner. The automatically extracted units can then be used as input for a bootstrapping procedure as described before.

Another precondition is the fact that structured activities are needed to define and apply a grammar. Here, the limitations are also clear as this concept is so far not extendable onto larger unrestricted video sets.

A possible solution in this context could be the usage of n-grams, e.g. bi- or tri-grams, instead of predefined grammars defining only possible transition to the next n states instead of complete activity paths. The predefined grammar in context of this work is needed to allow an evaluation, especially in terms of sequence accuracy. In case of real-world applications, this might not be feasible or desired. Therefore, is should be pointed out, that the assumption of a complete grammar, that has been made in the presented approach can easily be replaced by more handy concepts of n-grams by keeping a majority of the shown advantages.

The idea of using n-grams instead of predefined grammars is also related to the last point, the temporal span. The here proposed approach is able to cover several minutes of activities so far as see from the datasets used. This is of course a very limited time when it comes to real world data. Here also the main limiting factor is the application of a predefined grammar, which needs a start and end point to pass through a certain activity and again, a possible solution could be the application of other more flexible structure models.

6.2. Future Work

So far the proposed system mainly focuses on the human activity only. But as pointed out in the literature overview, there are many more cues that can come into play when it comes to the recognition of human actions like object knowledge or scene information.

One general advantage of the proposed generative approach is that it allows the integration of further cues, e.g. in terms of object state probabilities as they arise from action-object-complexes or the coupling with state probabilities based on global or local position information for known environments. This would add more information for example about currently handled objects at the lowest level, the unit recognition, by training additional mixture models handling the recognition of object features.

Another extension of the proposed approach would be the handling of parallel action units, for example if someone is stirring and pouring at the same time. As various types of HMM topology exists, including coupled

HMMs, the proposed system provides a natural way to handle such phenomenon.

This also holds for the case of human-human interaction. The modeling of such activity is still an open question in current research. In case of the here presented system, the combination of activities of different sources might be feasible by several parallel interacting instances.

Overall, the presented system can be seen as a first step towards a temporal analysis of human actions in video sequences. It is hoped that the provided results will be a basis for further developments and that the idea of the overall system in combination with the presented datasets will spur further research in this area.

A. Formal HMM notation

A.1. Sample HMM in HTK notation

This section shows an example for the notation of the HMM for the action unit "put bun together" from the breakfast datasets for an 30-dimensional input vector (based on 30 clusters). The notation is based on HTK definition of an HMM, listing first the mean and variance of the multivariate Gaussian mixture for each state and second the transition probability matrix for the related HMM. The transition probability matrix sows an upper bidiagonal form for the state two up to state seven, The first and the last state are the start resp. end state of the HMM and are therefore treated separately. The first state has only one transition to the next state and the last state does not have any outgoing transitions.

```
~h "put_bunTogether"
<BeginHMM>
  <NumStates> 8
  <State> 2
    <Mean> 30
      0.109264 0.061922 0.058748 ...
    <Variance> 30
      0.012750 0.006150 0.002454 ...
  <State> 3
    <Mean> 30
      0.048512 0.035177 0.030377 ...
    <Variance> 30
      0.004514 0.003314 0.002058 ...
  <State> 4
    <Mean> 30
      0.038673 0.030113 0.031311 ...
```

```
      <Variance> 30
        0.002675 0.001296 0.001187 ...
    <State> 5
      <Mean> 30
        0.024847 0.018266 0.033246 ...
      <Variance> 30
        0.001228 0.000782 0.001675 ...
    <State> 6
      <Mean> 30
        0.080568 0.049029 0.068198 ...
      <Variance> 30
        0.008836 0.006889 0.004633 ...
    <State> 7
      <Mean> 30
        0.112669 0.068833 0.048627 ...
      <Variance> 30
        0.025718 0.008317 0.004595 ...
    <TransP> 8
  0.0 1.00000 0.00000 0.00000 0.00000 0.00000
      0.00000 0.00000
  0.0 0.90554 0.09445 0.00000 0.00000 0.00000
      0.00000 0.00000
  0.0 0.00000 0.93853 0.06146 0.00000 0.00000
      0.00000 0.00000
  0.0 0.00000 0.00000 0.88500 0.11499 0.00000
      0.00000 0.00000
  0.0 0.00000 0.00000 0.00000 0.84096 0.15903
      0.00000 0.00000
  0.0 0.00000 0.00000 0.00000 0.00000 0.88353
      0.11646 0.00000
  0.0 0.00000 0.00000 0.00000 0.00000 0.00000
      0.91765 0.08234
  0.0 0.00000 0.00000 0.00000 0.00000 0.00000
      0.00000 0.00000
<EndHMM>
```

B. Grammar notation

B.1. Grammar for ADL dataset

This example shows the grammar of the ADL dataset. The notation follows the HTK specification (see [YEG+06]) based on EBNF form (see [Sta96]). Nonterminals are marked by a leading $ and are written in upper cases following the HTK grammar style. Terminals are represented by lower case strings.

```
$EAT_SNACK2 =  [move_hand_into_snackbox_lh]
     move_snack_to_mouth move_hand_from_mouth ;
$EAT_SNACK_END = move_hand_into_snackbox_lh [
     move_snack_to_mouth];
$SCROLL_PAGES = scroll_pages_to_left |
     scroll_pages_to_right ;

$ANSWER_PHONE = [move_hand_to_left] grab_phone
     open_phone_bh move_to_ear [use_phone] ;
$DIAL_PHONE =  [move_hand_to_left] grab_phone
     open_phone_bh dial_push_button move_to_ear
     use_phone ;
$EAT_BANANA =   [ (move_hand_to_left
     move_hand_to_right) ]  move_banana_to_mouth
     move_banana_down [peel_banana [peel_banana]]
     move_banana_to_mouth move_banana_down
     move_banana_to_mouth move_banana_down [
     move_banana_to_mouth [move_banana_down] ] ;
$CHOP_BANANA =   ((move_to_back_right
     turn_to_front_from_right[arrange_banana]) | (
     move_hand_to_right move_hand_to_left) )  cut
     cut [cut] [cut] [move_hand_to_right [
     move_hand_to_left]]  ;
```

```
$DRINK_WATER =    move_to_back_left open_fridge
    close_fridge turn_to_front_from_left [pick_glas
     | (move_hand_to_right move_hand_to_left)] pour
      place_bottle_onto_table [pick_glas |
    change_glas_to_other_hand] move_to_mouth drink
    [move_hand_from_mouth] ;
$EAT_SNACK =      [move_to_back] open_cupboard
    close_cupboard turn_to_front
    move_hand_into_snackbox_lh move_snack_to_mouth
    move_hand_from_mouth  $EAT_SNACK2 $EAT_SNACK2
    $EAT_SNACK2 [$EAT_SNACK2] [$EAT_SNACK_END] ;
$LOOKUP_IN_PHONEBOOK =   [move_to_back] open_drawer
     close_drawer turn_to_front
    place_book_on_table_rh open_book_bh
    $SCROLL_PAGES $SCROLL_PAGES $SCROLL_PAGES [
    $SCROLL_PAGES] [$SCROLL_PAGES] [$SCROLL_PAGES]
    search_entry ;
$PEEL_BANANA =   move_to_back turn_to_front
    peel_banana peel_banana [peel_banana] [
    peel_banana];
$USE_SILVERWARE =         move_to_back
    open_microwave close_microwave turn_to_front
    pick_up_silverware [arrange_silverware] cut [
    cut] [cut] [pick_up_food] move_fork_to_mouth [
    move_fork_from_mouth]   ;
$WRITE_ON_WHITEBORAD =   move_to_back_left
    write_on_whiteboard [turn_to_front_from_left] ;

$ACT = $ANSWER_PHONE |
$DIAL_PHONE |
$EAT_BANANA |
$CHOP_BANANA |
$DRINK_WATER |
$EAT_SNACK |
$LOOKUP_IN_PHONEBOOK |
$PEEL_BANANA |
$USE_SILVERWARE |
$WRITE_ON_WHITEBORAD ;
```

```
( [at_ease] $ACT [at_ease] )
```

B.2. Grammar for BKT dataset

This sections shows one possible sample grammar for the BKT dataset. Because of the simplicity of the involved activities, the grammar is flatter then the grammar of the ADL dataset.

```
$POURING = Schuessel_holen_fl Flasche_holen_fl
    Einschenken_fl Flasche_weglegen_fl
    Schuessel_weglegen_fl;
$STIRRING = Schuessel_holen_fl Kochloeffel_holen_fl
     Ruehren_fl Ruehren_fl Ruehren_fl [Ruehren_fl]
    [Ruehren_fl] Kochloeffel_weglegen_fl
    Schuessel_weglegen_fl;
$CUTTING = Apfel_holen_schneiden_fl Messer_holen_fl
     Apfel_greifen_linke_Hand_fl Schneiden_fl
    Schneiden_fl Schneiden_fl [Schneiden_fl]
    Apfel_loslassen_linke_Hand_fl
    Messer_weglegen_fl Apfel_weglegen_schneiden_fl;
$MASHING = Schuessel_holen_fl Stampfer_holen_fl
    Stampfen_fl Stampfen_fl Stampfen_fl Stampfen_fl
     [Stampfen_fl] Stampfer_weglegen_fl
    Schuessel_weglegen_fl;
$GRATING = Reibe_holen_fl Apfel_holen_fl Reiben_fl
    Reiben_fl Reiben_fl [Reiben_fl]
    Apfel_weglegen_fl Reiben_weglegen_fl;
$ROLLING = wellholz_holen_fl wellholz_greifen_fl
    auswellen_fl auswellen_fl auswellen_fl [
    auswellen_fl] wellholz_loslassen_fl
    wellholz_weglegen_fl;
$SLICING = hobel_holen_fl Apfel_holen_fl hobeln_fl
    hobeln_fl hobeln_fl hobeln_fl hobeln_fl [
    hobeln_fl] [hobeln_fl] [hobeln_fl]
    Apfel_weglegen_fl hobel_weglegen_fl;
$GRINDING = kaffeemuehle_holen_fl knauf_greifen_fl
    mahlen_fl mahlen_fl mahlen_fl [mahlen_fl] [
```

```
        mahlen_fl] knauf_loslassen_fl
        kaffemuehle_weglegen_fl;
$SWEEPING = Kehrbesteck_holen_beide_Haende_fl
        Kehren_fl Kehren_fl Kehren_fl [Kehren_fl] [
        Kehren_fl] [Kehren_fl]
        Kehrbesteck_weglegen_beide_Haende_fl;
$SAWING = Kuchen_holen_saegen_fl
        Saegemesser_holen_saegen_fl Saegen_fl Saegen_fl
         Saegen_fl [Saegen_fl] [Saegen_fl] [Saegen_fl]
        [Saegen_fl] Saegemesser_weglegen_saegen_fl
        Kuchen_weglegen_saegen_fl
        Kuchenstueck_weglegen_saegen_fl;

$ACT = $POURING |
$STIRRING |
$CUTTING |
$MASHING |
$GRATING |
$ROLLING |
$SLICING |
$GRINDING |
$SWEEPING |
$SAWING ;

([Rp] $ACT [Rp])
```

B.3. Grammar for ADL dataset

This sections shows an excerpt of the automatically build grammar for the Breakfast datasets. As the overall grammar with an overall of 256 nonterminals would be too complex to display, the excerpt shows only the possible unit combinations for the activity “preparing tea”. One can see that for the building process, all possible combinations of terminals are considered and represented by a nonterminal (line 2-9). The possible nonterminals correspond to the final activity (line 20). The definitions of other activities are omitted for clarity.

```
...
$TEA1 =  take_cup add_teabag pour_water  ;
$TEA2 =  add_teabag pour_water  ;
$TEA3 =  take_cup pour_water add_teabag  ;
$TEA4 =  pour_water add_teabag  ;
$TEA5 =  take_cup add_teabag pour_water spoon_sugar stir_tea  ;
$TEA6 =  add_teabag pour_water spoon_sugar stir_tea  ;
$TEA7 =  take_cup add_teabag pour_water spoon_sugar  ;
$TEA8 =  take_cup pour_water add_teabag pour_sugar  ;

$CEREALS = ...
$COFFEE = ...
$FRIEDEGG = ...
$JUICE = ...
$MILK = ...
$PANCAKE = ...
$SALAT = ...
$SANDWICH = ...
$SCRAMBLEDEGG = ...
$TEA = $TEA1 | $TEA2 | $TEA3 | $TEA4 | $TEA5 | $TEA6 | $TEA7 | $TEA8 ;

$ACT =  $CEREALS |
 $COFFEE |
 $FRIEDEGG |
 $JUICE |
 $MILK |
 $PANCAKE |
 $SALAT |
 $SANDWICH |
 $SCRAMBLEDEGG |
 $TEA ;

( [SIL] $ACT [SIL] )
```

List of Figures

List of Tables

Bibliography

[AAWD10] E. Aksoy, A. Abramov, F. Worgotter, and B. Dellen, "Categorizing object-action relations from semantic scene graphs," in *Proc. of IEEE International Conference on Robotics and Automation (ICRA)*, 2010, pp. 398–405.

[AC99] J. Aggarwal and Q. Cai, "Human Motion Analysis: A Review," *Computer Vision and Image Understanding (CVIU)*, vol. 73, no. 3, pp. 428 – 440, 1999.

[ARA^{+}06] T. Asfour, K. Regenstein, P. Azad, J. Schroder, A. Bierbaum, N. Vahrenkamp, and R. Dillmann, "ARMAR-III: An Integrated Humanoid Platform for Sensory-Motor Control," in *Proc. of IEEE-RAS International Conference on Humanoid Robots (HUMANOIDS)*, 2006, pp. 169–175.

[AV07] D. Arthur and S. Vassilvitskii, "K-means++: The Advantages of Careful Seeding," in *Proc. of ACM-SIAM Symposium on Discrete Algorithms (SODA)*, 2007, pp. 1027–1035.

[BB01] J. Baird and D. Baldwin, "Making Sense of Human Behavior: Action Parsing and Intentional Inference," in *Intentions and Intentionality*, F. Malle, L. Moses, and D. Baldwin, Eds. MIT Press, 2001, ch. 9.

[BBC13] BBC, "BBC NEWS | UK | The statistics of CCTV," sep 2013. [Online]. Available: http://news.bbc.co.uk/2/hi/uk_news/8159141.stm

[BC13] L. Breiman and A. Cutler, "Random Forests," sep 2013. [Online]. Available: http://stat-www.berkeley.edu/users/breiman/RandomForests/

[BD01] A. Bobick and J. Davis, "The recognition of human movement using temporal templates," *IEEE Transactions on Pattern Analysis and Machine Intelligence (PAMI)*, vol. 23, no. 3, pp. 257–267, 2001.

[Bel61] R. E. Bellman, *Adaptive control processes - A guided tour.* Princeton University Press, 1961.

[BGS$^+$05] M. Blank, L. Gorelick, E. Shechtman, M. Irani, and R. Basri, "Actions as space-time shapes," in *Proc. of IEEE International Conference on Computer Vision (ICCV)*, vol. 2, 2005, pp. 1395–1402.

[BK11] A. F. Bobick and V. Krüger, "On Human Action," in *Visual Analysis of Humans.* Springer Berlin Heidelberg, 2011, pp. 279–288.

[Bre01] L. Breiman, "Random Forests," *Machine Learning*, vol. 45, no. 1, pp. 5–32, 2001.

[CA11] C. Chen and J. Aggarwal, "Modeling human activities as speech," in *Proc. of IEEE Conference on Computer Vision and Pattern Recognition (CVPR)*, 2011, pp. 3425–3432.

[CBDF04] G. Csurka, C. Bray, C. Dance, and L. Fan, "Visual categorization with bags of keypoints," in *Proc. of the Workshop on Statistical Learning in Computer Vision (SLCV) at ECCV*, 2004, pp. 1–22.

[CBHK02] N. V. Chawla, K. W. Bowyer, L. O. Hall, and W. P. Kegelmeyer, "SMOTE: synthetic minority over-sampling technique,"

Journal of Artificial Intelligence Research (JAIR), vol. 16, no. 1, pp. 321 – 357, 2002.

[CCFC13] J. M. Chaquet, E. J. Carmona, and A. Fernandez-Caballero, "A survey of video datasets for human action and activity recognition," *Computer Vision and Image Understanding (CVIU)*, vol. 117, no. 6, pp. 633 – 659, 2013.

[CD00] R. Cutler and L. Davis, "Robust real-time periodic motion detection, analysis, and applications," *IEEE Transactions on Pattern Analysis and Machine Intelligence (PAMI)*, vol. 22, no. 8, pp. 781–796, 2000.

[CL93] T. F. Coleman and Y. Li, "An Interior Trust Region Approach for Nonlinear Minimization Subject to Bounds," Cornell University, Tech. Rep., 1993.

[CL11] C.-C. Chang and C.-J. Lin, "LIBSVM: A library for support vector machines," *ACM Transactions on Intelligent Systems and Technology (TIST)*, vol. 2, no. 3, pp. 27 – 27, 2011.

[Con13] L. D. Consortium, "LDC - Linguistic Data Consortium," sep 2013. [Online]. Available: http://www.ldc.upenn.edu/

[CP11] A. Chambolle and T. Pock, "A First-Order Primal-Dual Algorithm for Convex Problems with Applications to Imaging," *Journal of Mathematical Imaging and Vision (JMIV)*, vol. 40, no. 1, pp. 120 – 145, 2011.

[CSC+13] R. Chavarriaga, H. Sagha, A. Calatroni, S. T. Digumarti, G. Tröster, J. del R. Millán, and D. Roggen, "The Opportunity challenge: A benchmark database for on-body sensor-based activity recognition," *Pattern Recognition Letters*, vol. 34, no. 15, pp. 2033 – 2042, 2013.

[DT05] N. Dalal and B. Triggs, "Histograms of oriented gradients for human detection," in *Proc. of IEEE Conference on Computer Vision and Pattern Recognition (CVPR)*, 2005, pp. 886–893.

[EBMM03] A. Efros, A. Berg, G. Mori, and J. Malik, "Recognizing action at a distance," in *Proc. of IEEE International Conference on Computer Vision (ICCV)*, 2003, pp. 726–733.

[EG09] M. Enzweiler and D. Gavrila, "Monocular Pedestrian Detection: Survey and Experiments," *IEEE Transactions on Pattern Analysis and Machine Intelligence (PAMI)*, vol. 31, no. 12, pp. 2179–2195, 2009.

[FGMR10] P. Felzenszwalb, R. Girshick, D. McAllester, and D. Ramanan, "Object Detection with Discriminatively Trained Part-Based Models," *IEEE Transactions on Pattern Analysis and Machine Intelligence (PAMI)*, vol. 32, no. 9, pp. 1627–1645, 2010.

[FMR08] P. Felzenszwalb, D. McAllester, and D. Ramanan, "A discriminatively trained, multiscale, deformable part model," in *Proc. of IEEE Conference on Computer Vision and Pattern Recognition (CVPR)*, 2008, pp. 1–8.

[FR95] W. T. Freeman and M. Roth, "Orientation histograms for hand gesture recognition," in *Proc. of Workshop on Automatic Face- and Gesture-Recognition*, 1995.

[GFA12] G. Guerra-Filho and Y. Aloimonos, "The syntax of human actions and interactions ," *Journal of Neurolinguistics*, vol. 25, no. 5, pp. 500 – 514, 2012.

[GFFA05] G. Guerra-Filho, C. Fermüller, and Y. Aloimonos, "Discovering a language for human activity," in *Proc. of the AAAI Symposium on Anticipatory Cognitive Embodied Systems*, 2005.

[GHS11] A. Gaidon, Z. Harchaoui, and C. Schmid, "Actom Sequence Models for Efficient Action Detection," in *Proc. of IEEE Conference on Computer Vision and Pattern Recognition (CVPR)*, 2011, pp. 3201–3208.

[GKWS09] D. Gehrig, H. Kuehne, A. Woerner, and T. Schultz, "HMM-based human motion recognition with optical flow data," in *Proc. of IEEE-RAS International Conference on Humanoid Robots (HUMANOIDS)*, 2009, pp. 425–430.

[GLF+93] J. S. Garofolo, L. F. Lamel, W. M. Fisher, J. G. Fiscus, D. S. Pallett, and N. L. Dahlgren, "DARPA TIMIT Acoustic Phonetic Continuous Speech Corpus," 1993.

[GYG10] J. Gall, A. Yao, and L. V. Gool, "2D Action Recognition Serves 3D Human Pose Estimation," in *Proc. of European Conference on Computer Vision (ECCV)*, 2010, pp. 425–438.

[HCL03] C.-W. Hsu, C.-C. Chang, and C.-J. Lin, "A Practical Guide to Support Vector Classification," Department of Computer Science, National Taiwan University, Tech. Rep., 2003.

[HG09] H. He and E. A. Garcia, "Learning from Imbalanced Data," *IEEE Transactions on Knowledge and Data Engineering (TKDE)*, vol. 21, no. 9, pp. 1263–1284, 2009.

[HLD11] M. Hoai, Z. Lan, and F. De la Torre, "Joint Segmentation and Classification of Human Actions in Video," in *Proc. of IEEE Conference on Computer Vision and Pattern Recognition (CVPR)*, 2011, pp. 3265–3272.

[HS88] C. Harris and M. Stephens, "A Combined Corner and Edge Detector," in *Proc. of the Alvey Vision Conference*, 1988, pp. 147 – 151.

[IB00] Y. Ivanov and A. Bobick, "Recognition of visual activities and interactions by stochastic parsing," *IEEE Transactions on Pattern Analysis and Machine Intelligence (PAMI)*, vol. 22, no. 8, pp. 852–872, 2000.

[JDSP10] H. Jegou, M. Douze, C. Schmid, and P. Perez, "Aggregating local descriptors into a compact image representation," in *Proc. of IEEE Conference on Computer Vision and Pattern Recognition (CVPR)*, 2010, pp. 3304–3311.

[JJB13] M. Jain, H. Jegou, and P. Bouthemy, "Better exploiting motion for better action recognition," in *Proc. of IEEE Conference on Computer Vision and Pattern Recognition (CVPR)*, 2013, pp. 2555–2562.

[KG07] V. Krüger and D. Grest, "Using Hidden Markov Models for Recognizing Action Primitives in Complex Actions," in *Proc. of Scandinavian Conference on Image Analysis (SCIA)*, 2007, pp. 203–212.

[KGP+11] N. Krüger, C. Geib, J. Piater, R. Petrick, M. Steedman, F. Wörgötter, A. Ude, T. Asfour, D. Kraft, D. Omrčen, A. Agostini, and R. Dillmann, "Object Action Complexes: Grounded abstractions of sensory motor processes," *Robotics and Autonomous Systems*, vol. 59, no. 10, pp. 740 – 757, 2011.

[KGSS12] H. Kuehne, D. Gehrig, T. Schultz, and R. Stiefelhagen, "Online Action Recognition from sparse Feature Flow," in *Proc. of the International Conference on Computer Vision Theory and Applications (VISAPP)*, 2012.

[KJG+11] H. Kuehne, H. Jhuang, E. Garrote, T. Poggio, and T. Serre, "HMDB: A large video database for human motion recognition," in *Proc. of IEEE International Conference on Computer Vision (ICCV)*, 2011, pp. 2556–2563.

[KMS08] A. Kläser, M. Marszałek, and C. Schmid, "A Spatio-Temporal Descriptor Based on 3D-Gradients," in *Proc. of British Machine Vision Conference (BMVC)*, 2008, pp. 995 – 1004.

[KPFW08] H. Koehler, M. Pruzinec, T. Feldmann, and A. Woerner, "Automatic Human Model Parametrization From 3D Marker Data For Motion Recognition," in *Proc. of International Conference Computer Graphics, Visualization and Computer Vision (WSCG)*, 2008.

[KPH05] V. Kellokumpu, M. Pietikäinen, and J. Heikkilä, "Human Activity Recognition Using Sequences of Postures," in *Proc. of IAPR Conference on Machine Vision Applications (MVA)*, 2005, pp. 570–573.

[Krü06] V. Krüger, "Recognizing Action Primitives in Complex Actions Using Hidden Markov Models," in *Advances in Visual Computing*, 2006, pp. 538–547.

[KS13] H. Koppula and A. Saxena, "Anticipating Human Activities using Object Affordances for Reactive Robotic Response," in *Proc. of Robotics: Science and Systems Conference (RSS)*, 2013.

[Lap05] I. Laptev, "On Space-Time Interest Points," *International Journal of Computer Vision (IJCV)*, vol. 64, no. 2-3, pp. 107–123, 2005.

[LK81] B. Lucas and T. Kanade, "An iterative image registration technique with an application to stereo vision," in *Proc. of the International Joint Conference on Artificial Intelligence (IJCAI)*, 1981, pp. 674 – 679.

[LLS09] J. Liu, J. Luo, and M. Shah, "Recognizing Realistic Actions from Videos in the Wild," in *Proc. of IEEE International Conference on Computer Vision and Pattern Recognition (CVPR)*, 2009, pp. 1996–2003.

[LMSR08] I. Laptev, M. Marszalek, C. Schmid, and B. Rozenfeld, "Learning realistic human actions from movies," in *Proc. of IEEE Conference on Computer Vision and Pattern Recognition (CVPR)*, 2008, pp. 1–8.

[lTHM$^+$09] F. D. la Torre, J. Hodgins, J. Montano, S. Valcarcel, and J. Macey., "Guide to the Carnegie Mellon University Multimodal Activity (CMU-MMAC) Database," Robotics Institute, Carnegie Mellon University, Tech. Rep., 2009.

[lTHM$^+$13] F. D. la Torre, J. Hodgins, J. Montano, S. Valcarcel, R. Forcada, and J. Macey, "Quality of Life Grand Challenge | Kitchen Capture," Jun. 2013. [Online]. Available: http://kitchen.cs.cmu.edu

[Mac67] J. B. MacQueen, "Some Methods for Classification and Analysis of MultiVariate Observations," in *Proc. of the Berkeley Symposium on Mathematical Statistics and Probability*, vol. 1, 1967, pp. 281–297.

[MG01] T. B. Moeslund and E. Granum, "A Survey of Computer Vision-Based Human Motion Capture," *Computer Vision and Image Understanding (CVIU)*, vol. 81, no. 3, pp. 231 – 268, 2001.

[MHK06] T. B. Moeslund, A. Hilton, and V. Krüger, "A survey of advances in vision-based human motion capture and analysis," *Computer Vision and Image Understanding (CVIU)*, vol. 104, no. 2, pp. 90 – 126, 2006.

[MHS09] P. Matikainen, M. Hebert, and R. Sukthankar, "Trajectons: Action Recognition Through the Motion Analysis of Tracked Features," in *Proc. of the Workshop on Video-Oriented Object and Event Classification (VOEC) at ICCV*, 2009.

[MHS10] ——, "Representing Pairwise Spatial and Temporal Relations for Action Recognition," in *Proc. of European Conference on Computer Vision (ECCV)*, 2010, pp. 508–521.

[MLS09] M. Marszalek, I. Laptev, and C. Schmid, "Actions in context," in *Proc. of IEEE Conference on Computer Vision and Pattern Recognition (CVPR)*, 2009, pp. 2929–2936.

[MPK09] R. Messing, C. Pal, and H. Kautz, "Activity recognition using the velocity histories of tracked keypoints," in *Proc. of IEEE International Conference on Computer Vision (ICCV)*, 2009, pp. 104–111.

[NCFF10] J. C. Niebles, C.-W. Chen, and L. Fei-Fei, "Modeling temporal structure of decomposable motion segments for activity classification," in *Proc. of European Conference on Computer Vision (ECCV)*, 2010, pp. 392 – 405.

[ORBD08] S. M. Oh, J. M. Rehg, T. Balch, and F. Dellaert, "Learning and Inferring Motion Patterns using Parametric Segmental Switching Linear Dynamic Systems," *International Journal of Computer Vision (IJCV)*, vol. 77, no. 1-3, pp. 103 – 124, 2008.

[ORBD13] ——, "Parametric Segmental Switching Linear Dynamic Systems (SLDSs)," aug 2013. [Online]. Available: http://www.cc.gatech.edu/~borg/ijcv_psslds/

[Ots79] N. Otsu, "A Threshold Selection Method from Gray-Level Histograms," *IEEE Transactions on Systems, Man and Cybernetics*, vol. 9, no. 1, pp. 62–66, 1979.

[PA04] S. Park and J. Aggarwal, "A hierarchical Bayesian network for event recognition of human actions and interactions," *Multimedia Systems*, vol. 10, no. 2, pp. 164–179, 2004.

[Pop10] R. Poppe, "A survey on vision-based human action recognition," *Image and Vision Computing*, vol. 28, no. 6, pp. 976 – 990, 2010.

[PR14] H. Pirsiavash and D. Ramanan, "Parsing videos of actions with segmental grammars," in *Proc. of IEEE Conference on Computer Vision and Pattern Recognition (CVPR)*, 2014.

[RA09] M. S. Ryoo and J. K. Aggarwal, "Semantic Representation and Recognition of Continued and Recursive Human Activities," *International Journal of Computer Vision (IJCV)*, vol. 82, no. 1, pp. 1–24, 2009.

[RA10] ——, "UT-Interaction Dataset, ICPR contest on Semantic Description of Human Activities (SDHA)," 2010. [Online]. Available: http://cvrc.ece.utexas.edu/SDHA2010/Human_Interaction.html

[RAAS12] M. Rohrbach, S. Amin, M. Andriluka, and B. Schiele, "A Database for Fine Grained Activity Detection of Cooking Activities," in *Proc. of IEEE Conference on Computer Vision and Pattern Recognition (CVPR)*, 2012, pp. 1194–1201.

[Rab89] L. Rabiner, "A tutorial on hidden markov models and selected applications in speech recognition," *Proceedings of the IEEE*, vol. 77, no. 2, pp. 257–286, 1989.

[RAS08] M. Rodriguez, J. Ahmed, and M. Shah, "Action MACH a spatio-temporal Maximum Average Correlation Height filter for action recognition," in *Proc. of IEEE Conference on Computer Vision and Pattern Recognition (CVPR)*, 2008, pp. 1–8.

[RCR+13] D. Roggen, A. Calatroni, M. Rossi, T. Holleczek, K. Förster, G. Tröster, P. Lukowicz, D. Bannach, G. Pirkl, A. Ferscha, J. Doppler, C. Holzmann, M. Kurz, G. Holl, R. Chavarriaga, H. Sagha, H. Bayati, M. Creatura, and J. del R. Millan, "OPPORTUNITY Activity Recognition Data Set," jun 2013. [Online]. Available: http://www.opportunity-project.eu/challengeDataset

[RJ86] L. Rabiner and B. Juang, "An introduction to hidden Markov models," *IEEE Acoustics, Speech and Signal Processing Magazine (ASSP)*, vol. 3, no. 1, pp. 4–16, 1986.

[Roh13] M. Rohrbach, "MPII Cooking Activities Dataset," jun 2013. [Online]. Available: http://www.d2.mpi-inf.mpg.de/mpii-cooking

[RS10] M. Raptis and S. Soatto, "Tracklet descriptors for action modeling and video analysis," in *Proc. of European conference on Computer vision (ECCV)*, 2010, pp. 577 – 590.

[RSAHS14] L. Rybok, B. Schauerte, Z. Al-Halah, and R. Stiefelhagen, ""Important Stuff, Everywhere!" Activity Recognition with Salient Proto-Objects as Context," in *Proc. IEEE Winter Conference on Applications of Computer Vision (WACV)*, Steamboat Springs, CO, USA, March 24-26 2014.

[Ryo11] M. S. Ryoo, "Human activity prediction: Early recognition of ongoing activities from streaming videos," in *Proc. of IEEE International Conference on Computer Vision (ICCV)*, 2011, pp. 1036–1043.

[RYS02] C. Rao, A. Yilmaz, and M. Shah, "View-Invariant Representation and Recognition of Actions," *International Journal of Computer Vision (IJCV)*, vol. 50, no. 2, pp. 203–226, 2002.

[SAS07] P. Scovanner, S. Ali, and M. Shah, "A 3-dimensional sift descriptor and its application to action recognition," in *Proc. of the ACM International Conference on Multimedia (ACM MM)*, 2007, pp. 357 – 360.

[Sch97] F. Schiel, "A Tutorial to HTK," International Computer Science Institute, Berkeley, Tech. Rep., 1997. [Online]. Available: http://www.bas.uni-muenchen.de/forschung/publikationen/Schiel_HTK.txt

[SDH09] E. H. Spriggs, F. De la Torre, and M. Hebert, "Temporal Segmentation and Activity Classification from First-person Sensing," in *Proc. of IEEE Workshop on Egocentric Vision at CVPR*, June 2009.

[SFC$^+$11] J. Shotton, A. Fitzgibbon, M. Cook, T. Sharp, M. Finocchio, R. Moore, A. Kipman, and A. Blake, "Real-time human pose recognition in parts from single depth images," in *Proc. of IEEE Conference on Computer Vision and Pattern Recognition (CVPR)*, 2011, pp. 1297 – 1304.

[SJLZ12] L. Shao, L. Ji, Y. Liu, and J. Zhang, "Human action segmentation and recognition via motion and shape analysis," *Pattern Recognition Letters*, vol. 33, no. 4, pp. 438 – 445, 2012.

[SKD$^+$13] A. Shimada, K. Kondo, D. Deguchi, G. Morin, and H. Stern, "Kitchen Scene Context based Gesture Recognition, ICPR 2012 Contest," Jun. 2013. [Online]. Available: http://www.murase.m.is.nagoya-u.ac.jp/KSCGR/

[SKLM05a] C. Sminchisescu, A. Kanaujia, Z. Li, and D. Metaxas, "Conditional models for contextual human motion recognition," in *Proc. of IEEE International Conference on Computer Vision (ICCV)*, 2005, pp. 1808–1815.

[SKLM05b] ——, "Discriminative density propagation for 3D human motion estimation," in *Proc. of IEEE Conference on Computer Vision and Pattern Recognition (CVPR)*, vol. 1, 2005, pp. 390–397.

[SLC04] C. Schuldt, I. Laptev, and B. Caputo, "Recognizing human actions: a local SVM approach," in *Proc. of the International Conference on Pattern Recognition (ICPR)*, vol. 3, 2004, pp. 32–36.

[Sor10] L. Sorber, "k-means++ - File Exchange - MATLAB Central," Sep. 2010. [Online]. Available: http://www.mathworks.com/matlabcentral/fileexchange/28804-k-means++

[ST94] J. Shi and C. Tomasi, "Good features to track," in *Proc. of IEEE Conference on Computer Vision and Pattern Recognition (CVPR)*, 1994, pp. 593–600.

[Sta96] E. S. S. Standard, "EBNF: ISO/IEC 14977 : 1996(E) Information Technology - Syntactic Metalanguage - Extended BNF," International Organization for Standardization, Tech. Rep., 1996.

[SWY75] G. Salton, A. Wong, and C. S. Yang, "A Vector Space Model for Automatic Indexing," *Communications of the ACM*, vol. 18, no. 11, pp. 613–620, 1975.

[TBB09] M. Tenorth, J. Bandouch, and M. Beetz, "The TUM Kitchen Data Set of Everyday Manipulation Activities for Motion Tracking and Action Recognition," in *Proc. of IEEE International Workshop on Tracking Humans for the Evaluation of their Motion in Image Sequences (THEMIS) at ICCV*, 2009.

[TBB13] ——, "TUM Ktichen Dataset," Jun. 2013. [Online]. Available: http://ias.in.tum.de/software/kitchen-activity-data

[TCSU08] P. Turaga, R. Chellappa, V. S. Subrahmanian, and O. Udrea, "Machine Recognition of Human Activities: A Survey," *IEEE Transactions on Circuits and Systems for Video Technology*, vol. 18, no. 11, pp. 1473–1488, 2008.

[Teo13] C. L. Teo, "UMD Sushi-Making Dataset," Aug. 2013. [Online]. Available: http://www.umiacs.umd.edu/research/POETICON/umd_sushi/t

[TYD+12] C. Teo, Y. Yang, H. Daume, C. Fermuller, and Y. Aloimonos, "Towards a Watson that sees: Language-guided action recognition for robots," in *Proc. of IEEE International Conference on Robotics and Automation (ICRA)*, 2012, pp. 374–381.

[VA13] S. Vishwakarma and A. Agrawal, "A survey on activity recognition and behavior understanding in video surveillance," *The Visual Computer*, vol. 29, no. 10, pp. 983–1009, 2013.

[WKSL11] H. Wang, A. Kläser, C. Schmid, and C.-L. Liu, "Action recognition by dense trajectories," in *Proc. of IEEE Conference on Computer Vision and Pattern Recognition (CVPR)*, 2011, pp. 3169–3176.

[WMS10] S. Wu, B. E. Moore, and M. Shah, "Chaotic invariants of Lagrangian particle trajectories for anomaly detection in crowded scenes," in *Proc. of IEEE Conference on Computer Vision and Pattern Recognition (CVPR)*, 2010, pp. 2054–2060.

[WOS11] S. Wu, O. Oreifej, and M. Shah, "Action recognition in videos acquired by a moving camera using motion decomposition of Lagrangian particle trajectories," in *Proc. of IEEE International Conference on Computer Vision (ICCV)*, 2011, pp. 1419–1426.

[WRB06] D. Weinland, R. Ronfard, and E. Boyer, "Free viewpoint action recognition using motion history volumes," *Computer Vision and Image Understanding (CVIU)*, vol. 104, no. 2, pp. 249 – 257, 2006.

[WRB11] ——, "A survey of vision-based methods for action representation, segmentation and recognition," *Computer Vision and Image Understanding (CVIU)*, vol. 115, no. 2, pp. 224 – 241, 2011.

[WTv08] G. Willems, T. Tuytelaars, and L. van Gool, "An Efficient Dense and Scale-Invariant Spatio-Temporal Interest Point Detector," in *Proc. of European Conference on Computer Vision (ECCV)*, 2008, pp. 650–663.

[WUK+09] H. Wang, M. M. Ullah, A. Kläser, I. Laptev, and C. Schmid, "Evaluation of local spatio-temporal features for action recognition," in *Proc. of British Machine Vision Conference (BMVC)*, 2009, pp. 124.1–124.11.

[YEG+06] S. J. Young, G. Evermann, M. J. F. Gales, T. Hain, D. Kershaw, G. Moore, J. Odell, D. Ollason, D. Povey, V. Valtchev, and P. C. Woodland, *The HTK Book, version 3.4*. Cambridge University Engineering Department, 2006.

[You13] YouTube, LLC, "Charts - YouTube," Sep. 2013. [Online]. Available: http://www.youtube.com/charts/videos_views?t=a

[YRT89] S. Young, N. Russell, and J. Thornton, "Token passing: a simple conceptual model for connected speech recognition systems," Cambridge University, Tech. Rep., 1989.

[ZDH13] F. Zhou, F. De la Torre, and J. Hodgins, "Hierarchical Aligned Cluster Analysis for Temporal Clustering of Human Motion,"

IEEE Transactions on Pattern Analysis and Machine Intelligence (PAMI), vol. 35, no. 3, pp. 582–596, 2013.

[ZF03] B. Zitova and J. Flusser, "Image registration methods: a survey." *Image Vision Comput.*, vol. 21, no. 11, pp. 977–1000, 2003.

[ZFFX11] B. Zhao, L. Fei-Fei, and E. P. Xing, "Online detection of unusual events in videos via dynamic sparse coding," in *Proc. of IEEE Conference on Computer Vision and Pattern Recognition (CVPR)*, 2011.

[ZKAM09] J. M. Zacks, S. Kumar, R. A. Abrams, and R. Mehta, "Using movement and intentions to understand human activity," *Cognition, International Journal of Cognitive Science*, vol. 112, no. 2, pp. 201 – 216, 2009.

[ZSS+07] J. M. Zacks, N. K. Speer, K. M. Swallow, T. S. Braver, and J. R. Reynolds, "Event perception: a mind-brain perspective," *Psychological bulletin*, vol. 133, no. 2, pp. 273 – 293, 2007.

[ZSV04] H. Zhong, J. Shi, and M. Visontai, "Detecting unusual activity in video," in *Proc. of IEEE Conference on Computer Vision and Pattern Recognition (CVPR)*, 2004.

[ZTH11] Z. Zhang, T. Tan, and K. Huang, "An Extended Grammar System for Learning and Recognizing Complex Visual Events," *IEEE Transactions on Pattern Analysis and Machine Intelligence (PAMI)*, vol. 33, no. 2, pp. 240–255, 2011.

Publications

[BK09] A. Bachmann and H. Kuehne, "An Iterative Scheme for Motion-Based Scene Segmentation," in *Proc. of Workshop on Dynamical Vision (DV) at ICCV*, 2009.

[BKG+06] I. Boesnach, H. Koehler, D. Gehrig, G. Stelzner, C. Simonidis, A. Fischer, and T. Stein., "A large-scale database of human movements to humanize robot motion," in *Proc. of French-German Workshop on Humanoid and Legged Robots (HLR)*, 2006.

[DGK+08] M. Do, D. Gehrig, H. Kuehne, P. Azad, P. Pastor, T. Asfour, T. Schultz, A. Woerner, and R. Dillmann, "Transfer of Human Movements to Humanoid Robots," in *Proc. of Workshop on Imitation and Coaching in Humanoid Robots at Humanoids*, 2008.

[GFK+08] D. Gehrig, A. Fischer, H. Kuehne, T. Stein, A. Woerner, H. Schwameder, and T. Schultz, "Online Recognition of Daily-Life Movements," in *Proc. of Workshop on Imitation and Coaching in Humanoid Robots at Humanoids*, 2008.

[GKR+11] D. Gehrig, P. Krauthausen, L. Rybok, H. Kuehne, U. D. Hanebeck, T. Schultz, and R. Stiefelhagen, "Combined intention, activity, and motion recognition for a humanoid household robot," in *Proc. of IEEE/RSJ Conference on Intelligent Robots and Systems (IROS)*, 2011, pp. 4819–4825.

[GKWS09] D. Gehrig, H. Kuehne, A. Woerner, and T. Schultz, "HMM-based Human Motion Recognition with Optical Flow Data," in *Proc. of IEEE Conference on Humanoid Robots (HUMANOIDS)*, 2009, pp. 425–430.

[KBPC04] H. Koehler, S. Bouattour, D. Paulus, and M. Couprie, "Analyse des Herzkranzgefäßbaums für die prä- und post-operative Diagnose," in *Proc. des Workshops Bildverarbeitung für die Medizin (BVM)*, 2004, pp. 269–273.

[KCBP04] H. Koehler, M. Couprie, S. Bouattour, and D. Paulus, "Extraction and analysis of coronary tree from single x-ray angiographies," in *Proc. of SPIE International Symposium Medical Imaging*, vol. 5367, 2004, pp. 810–819.

[KGSS12] H. Kuehne, D. Gehrig, T. Schultz, and R. Stiefelhagen, "Online Action Recognition from sparse Feature Flow," in *Proc. of International Conference on Computer Vision Theory and Applications (VISAPP)*, 2012, pp. 634–639.

[KJG+11] H. Kuehne, H. Jhuang, E. Garrote, T. Poggio, and T. Serre, "HMDB: a large video database for human motion recognition," in *Proceedings of IEEE International Conference on Computer Vision (ICCV)*, 2011, pp. 2556–2563.

[KPFW08] H. Koehler, M. Pruzinec, T. Feldmann, and A. Woerner, "Automatic Human Model Parametrization From 3D Marker Data For Motion Recognition," in *Proc. of International Conference on Computer Graphics, Visualization and Computer Vision (WSCG)*, 2008.

[KW08] H. Koehler and A. Woerner., "Motion-based Feature Tracking For Articulated Motion Analysis," in *Proc. of Workshop on*

Multimodal Interactions Analysis of Users a Controlled Environment (MIAUCE) at ICMI, 2008.

[KW09] H. Kuehne and A. Woerner, "Motion-based Feature Clustering for Articulated Body Tracking," in *Proc. of International Conference on Computer Vision Theory and Applications (VISAPP)*, 2009, pp. 579–584.

[KW10] ——, "Motion Segmentation of Articulated Structures by Integration of Visual Perception Criteria," in *Proc. of International Conference on Computer Vision Theory and Applications (VISAPP)*, 2010, pp. 54–59.

[KWP05] H. Koehler, T. Wittenberg, and D. Paulus, "Detection and Segmentation of Cervical Cell Nuclei," in *Biomedizinische Technik*, 2005, pp. 588–589.

[PKW08] M. Pruzinec, H. Koehler, and A. Woerner, "Localisation of Joint Rotation Centres for 3D Human Motion Simulation," in *Proc. of European Simulation and Modelling Conference (ESM)*, 2008.

[SFB+07] T. Stein, A. Fischer, I. Boesnach, D. Gehrig, H. Koehler, and H. Schwameder, "Kinematische Analyse menschlicher Alltagsbewegungen für die Mensch-Maschine-Interaktion," in *Sporttechnologie zwischen Theorie und Praxis, V*, 2007.